LIVING WITH ENERGY SHORTFALL

Also of Interest

† Available in hardcover and paperback.

About the Book and Author

Living with Energy Shortfall:
A Future for American Towns and Cities
Jon Van Til

The specter of a permanent energy crunch looms larger in the United States each year. Oil supplies, though vast, are not infinite and are rapidly escalating in cost; oil shale development is protested by environmentalists and may be limited by scanty water resources in western states; widespread use of nuclear energy—once assumed to be the panacea for all energy problems—now looks socially and economically questionable; and solar and other renewable energy resources remain in the early stages of development. Extensive energy conservation, it becomes increasingly clear, cannot entirely resolve the energy dilemma. And it is equally clear that a permanent energy shortfall will have a tremendous impact on our way of life—on where, as well as on how, we live.

In this very timely book, Jon Van Til argues that we must rethink the future of our cities so that the most efficient use can be made of the limited energy supplies still available. Today's residential patterns —typified by urban sprawl and heavy commuter traffic—cannot, he is sure, continue in the face of increasingly expensive and scarce fuel supplies. Dr. Van Til suggests alternative forms that our cities and suburbs might assume, given three possible energy scenarios, and explores emerging methods of energy conservation and coproduction that may insulate us from the ravages of energy dislocation. He is convinced, however, that densely populated areas made up of "minicities" in which people live near their work places are essential to any energy-efficient future.

Jon Van Til is an associate professor and chairman of the Department of Urban Studies and Community Development at the Rutgers University Camden College. He is coauthor of *Privilege in America: An End to Inequality?* (1973), has published leading papers on energy futures and is editor-in-chief of the *Journal of Voluntary Action Research*.

TO WILLIAM VAN TIL
teacher, editor, colleague, and father

Rarely has one done more to merit a book's dedication

Jon Van Til

LIVING WITH ENERGY SHORTFALL
A Future for American Towns and Cities

Westview Press
Boulder, Colorado

This book is based on a number of previously published works of the author, who gratefully acknowledges the copyright permission given by the Aid Association for Lutherans, the *Journal of the American Planning Association, The Futurist,* and Pergamon Press.

Published in 1982 in the United States of America by
Westview Press, Inc.
5500 Central Avenue
Boulder, Colorado 80301
Frederick A. Praeger, President and Publisher

Library of Congress Catalog Card Number 82- 50611
ISBN 0-86531-135-8
ISBN 0-86531-136-6 (pbk)

Printed and bound in the United States of America

Contents

Figures and Tables

Foreword

Jon Van Til's book is written for the ultimate energy policy maker–the private citizen. Since its first writing we have experienced an "oil glut" and become aware of vast new supplies of natural gas at depths previously beyond drilling range. Those facts might cause some readers to wonder if Van Til's conclusions are exaggerated. Maybe we don't need to change our ways so much, and maybe we have more time in which to do it.

Actually, it is when the U.S. energy situation, which Van Til writes about, is seen in its global context that the true dimensions of the dilemma begin to emerge. Modern industrial society is designed to run on petroleum and natural gas. Massive road-building dwarfs all other public works; automobile production is central to the economies of the most highly industrialized nations. An enormous chemical industry depends upon natural gas as its basic raw material. Only England and West Germany among industrialized countries derive less than two-thirds of their energy needs from oil and gas. As earlier societies had been shaped by the advent of new energy sources–draft animals, sailing ships, waterwheels, coal–so modern industrial society is shaped by its energy sources. Urbanization and agribusiness alike depend upon cheap, easily transportable liquid and gaseous fuels.

For two decades after World War II, it was more or less assumed that the newly liberated colonies, the new countries of the Third World, would follow in the same pattern. The trail had been blazed by the United States and a few others; the "stages of growth" were to be achieved in succession, more rapidly than the industrialized nations had passed through them. Little thought was given in those days to the possibility that energy and other resources might prove to be a limitation.

Although estimates vary tremendously, the total energy potentially available in fossil fuels around the world is probably something of the order of 10^{23} joules (one joule, the international unit of energy measurement, is equal to one watt per second). Of this, about two-thirds is in the form of coal and lignite. Around a fifth is petroleum and natural gas, and something like another fifth is heavy oil, oil shale, and tar sands. Of the total world supply of recoverable fossil-fuel energy, approximately 1/400 is used up every year at the present rate. More than two-thirds of the present use is oil and gas; most of this is used in industrialized countries.

During the past quarter-century, world fuel consumption tripled, oil and gas consumption quintupled, and electricity use grew nearly sevenfold. Even though these rates of increase have dropped off somewhat as energy prices have risen, if the countries of the Third World are to develop industrially, their energy consumption will rise accordingly.

World oil production will turn downward in the next ten to twenty years, and there will be severe regional shortages before that. World natural gas production, even with the new deep-level finds, will peak out within only a few decades. The other fossil fuels pose severe environmental problems both in their extraction and combustion.

The energy crisis in the Third World is even more severe than that in the industrialized nations. Traditional energy sources—principally firewood, charcoal, and forage for draft animals—are growing scarce and expensive. Where ecological carrying capacities have been exceeded, forests are receding and grasslands are becoming deserts. Third World deforestation is advancing rapidly, and with it the erosion of topsoil; still further problems result when deforestation and subsequent erosion silt reservoirs. Dependence of developing countries on world oil supplies has been increasing, and these countries are in a poorer position than the industrialized nations to absorb or offset the adverse economic impacts of rising oil prices.

Not too long ago it was widely assumed that nuclear technologies would be available to take over energy supply functions as oil supplies began to give out. As is well known, it turns out that nuclear fission and breeder technologies lack public acceptance on safety grounds, and fusion power will apparently not be available nearly as soon, nor as cheaply, nor as "cleanly" as was expected.

Solar energy, including solar electricity and high-temperature heat, is already economically competitive in much of the Third World; it compares less favorably with conventional energy sources in the industrialized world. But to shift to major dependence on solar energy would require massive capital investment and many years.

We can summarize the world energy situation in three statements:

1. The industrialized world is in a transition *from* high and growing per-capita consumption of energy, predominantly from oil
   and natural gas, *to* lower per-capita energy consumption,
   coming to an increasing extent from renewable sources. This
   transition involves a major restructuring, whole-system change,
   not simply a change in energy practice and policies. It will
   come about not because of an exhaustion of either fossil or
   nuclear fuels, but because of high social and environmental
   costs of continuing present trends, together with mounting
   pressure from the majority populations (and a majority of nations) of the world who are not yet industrialized.
2. The developing world will not have the energy available to
   develop in the pattern of the present industrialized world. Not
   just because of energy limitations, but because of other
   resource and environmental constraints as well, the Third
   World will *never* have the material standard of living presently
   enjoyed in the United States, let alone the standard Americans
   may have aspired to.
3. There is rapidly growing awareness of these facts. Either the
   Third World and the industrial world will join in partnership to
   create a new global order in which this disparity is dealt with,
   or there will be increasing and increasingly unpleasant con-
   frontations between the developed and the developing countries. As the recent Brandt Commission Report, *North-South: A
   Program for Survival,* summarized the situation, there cannot
   be world peace when there is mass poverty and when the existing global order is perceived by a large fraction of the
   world's population as fundamentally inequitable.

Jon Van Til's thesis acquires additional urgency and pungency
when viewed against this background. If the world condition were
not what it is, the United States would still be finding it necessary to
change its profligate way of life, as in fact it has been doing for some
half dozen years in some degree. In the context of the global situation
outlined above, the energy behavior of the United States and other
industrialized nations becomes critical. And the critical choosing, as
Van Til points out, will be done not in Washington, Houston, or
Riyadh, but by the individual consumer of energy and energy-
embodying products. Perhaps for that reason, there is a chance the
choosing may be done well.

Willis W. Harman

Acknowledgments

This book began to take form in the cold Philadelphia winter of 1977–1978. It was nurtured by colleagues at Rutgers University: Dean Walter K. Gordon supported a year's faculty study leave; Professors Rita Mae Kelly, Michael H. Lang, and Raphael J. Salmon encouraged my work and read early drafts of papers I began writing on urban energy futures.

My sabbatical at the Institute of Behavioral Science at the University of Colorado nurtured my thinking and work. The colleagueship of Kenneth Boulding, Spenser Havlick, Betsy Moen, Paul Wehr, Lou McClelland, and Jerrold Krenz expanded my vision. Stuart Cook proved a gracious institutional host to his visiting scholar.

Journal editors were helpful in focusing my writing, especially Kenneth Pearlman of the *Journal of the American Planning Association* and Jerry Richardson of *The Futurist*. More recently, Oktay Ural and Ira Robinson have encouraged publication of my papers at several international conferences.

Colleagues nationwide have been helpful and supportive. Peter Pollock, until recently of the Solar Energy Research Institute and Riley Dunlap at Washington State University have proved invaluable as networkers and readers; their enthusiasm has been the source of much encouragement. Stephen Weiner and Robert P. Culleton, long-time friends, also provided supportive reading and advice, as did Roy Van Til, economist and futurist at Bentley College.

At Westview Press, Miriam Gilbert has been a marvelous managing editor, full of good ideas and good cheer, and unwavering in her support. Alice Levine, Dorothy Merrifield, and Jeanne Remington edited the manuscript with great competence and sensitivity to what I was trying to say. Fred Praeger supported the original concept of the book with an enthusiasm that has been highly gratifying.

Westview's reader, Langdon Crane, was everything a reader should be: intelligent, critical, highly informed, and very helpful to me in preparing the final draft.

Jon Novak, Neil Hatcher, and Professor John Gagliardi read several chapters; their comments were carefully heeded and very much appreciated. Another fellow warrior in the social politics of southern New Jersey, Al Wilson, provided great colleagueship as we developed the Conference on Energy Choices in 1981. Ann Birney played a crucial role as graduate student and colleague in developing the research base that underlies Chapter 4.

Ruby Fulk typed two drafts of the manuscript with the promptness, accuracy, and good cheer that have made her a Boulder legend. Anna Lorang typed many of the final chapters. Sandra Cheesman provided secretarial support throughout the project, and her enthusiasm and interest mark her as a delightful and productive colleague.

My family grew up during this project. Ross, now four, learned to crawl, walk, talk, and think. His faith that "the publisher will like it" has been unwavering. Claire, now two, learned many skills during this time as well and never disrupted a pile of papers she learned to call "Daddy book."

Dr. Trudy Heller did what every modern wife should do when her husband writes a book: She wrote her own book and got it finished and published more quickly. Like her, I do not regret a moment of the many hours of child care we divided while the two projects advanced to their completion.

Finally, my parents did what they have always done when one of their children strove to complete a major project. They maintained an unflagging interest in its progress and provided much useful advice when it was requested. In addition, William Van Til performed a detailed and expert reading and editing of the entire draft, and Beatrice Van Til provided invaluable advice regarding Chapter 6. Few authors have parents more able, concerned, and supportive than I have been blessed with.

I deeply appreciate the help, colleagueship, enthusiasm, and support of those I have named. The book's flaws remain mine, but its strong points I gladly share with my network.

Jon Van Til

Introduction

This book is about the ways Americans may live in the years ahead and the forms our cities, suburbs, towns, and rural areas may take in the light of changing patterns of energy supply and societal affluence. It is a foray into the urban sociology of the future and an effort to discern patterns by which we may cope with those basic deter-minants of the shape of our landscape—energy, communications, production, and the quest for amenities.

Of these four factors that shape the spatial patterns in which our homes, places of work, schools, and centers of culture are arranged, energy is a primary factor and always has been. The other factors cer-tainly make their mark on these patterns, but it is energy that most fundamentally enables and constrains our use of urban, suburban, and rural space.

The argument of the book is developed in three stages, paralleling Sheridan's venerable saw regarding the construction of his plays. In the first act, the playwright is said to have remarked, he chases the protagonist up a tree; in the second act, he throws rocks at him; and in the third act, the protagonist is extricated from his precarious perch by the author.

We are already treed by forces of energy limitation, resource ex-haustion, and economic adversity. Chapters 1, 2, and 3 detail that predicament and demonstrate the plausibility of three possible scenarios for the years ahead. None is much better than our recent past, and two are distinctly more troublesome.

In the second section of this book, the way we live in geographic space is considered. Urban, suburban, and nonmetropolitan spatial forms are discussed in Chapter 4, and the impact of possible energy patterns upon those forms is considered in Chapter 5. The final chapter (6) in this section presents my best guesses as to what the future of these patterns is likely to be.

The "third act" considers means by which we may extricate ourselves from that part of our energy problem that is worsened by the spatial patterns in which we have come to live. The concept of "coproduction" is presented in Chapter 7 as a key to the development of personal, community, and even national energy independence (at least in part). Survey data are searched for cues in Chapter 8 to indicate the readiness of Americans for the changes in energy patterns that likely await them.

The book closes with a brief epilogue in which the reader is invited to apply the conclusions of the book to his or her own life, values, and future. Several exercises are presented to assist in the projection of personal futures – of images of the way we may live in the years ahead.

No author is without biases or preferences, and the present writer should confess to his. By academic training I am a sociologist; by professional experience an administrator, teacher, and program developer; and by preference a writer and futurist. My politics are democratic, distributive, participatory, and pragmatic. I prefer voluntary action to compulsory solutions and distrust large institutions, whether corporate or governmental, that are not subject to the control of their participant members. I view the world as a "guarded pessimist." I have a great faith in the power and wisdom of citizen enlightenment.

However, the future cannot be precisely discerned. I therefore find it prudent to avoid flat predictions and to seek instead to develop alternative futures for consideration. I seek to be as objective as possible in describing these futures. Nevertheless, the values that underlie my conceptions of future goods and evils surely provide an element of subjectivity to which the reader might choose to respond by clarifying his or her own preferences about the future of the United States.

Ultimately, I am convinced that the choices of individuals, in the contexts of their families and communities, will make a great deal of difference in our energy future. To be sure, such factors as corporate policy, resource availability, and international hostility will also be critical. But choices remain before us that permit the development of a quite considerable cushion of energy independence – for families, neighborhoods, cities, and the nation at large. If these choices are recognized and made while the opportunity provides, our future will be far more likely to resemble the level of comfort that has characterized our recent past. But, if these choices are clouded and foregone, so will we forego opportunities of self-determination and self-preservation that may be impossible to recapture.

So this book is really about choices—choices of residence, community, modes of transportation, and patterns of energy use. And these choices, as made by all of us in the years immediately ahead, will have a substantial impact on the way we shall live in the future. These choices, in a very real sense, are ours alone to make, and are of enormous importance.

1

Energy, Ideology, and Shortfall

Let us begin not with an image of the present or future city, but rather with a picture of a city form long thought to be abandoned by civilized societies. Drawing its images in some detail will help us see what cities and other spatial settlements may be like under differing conditions of energy availability and affluence. Is this simply the image of a city discarded with the rise of the industrial city, or does it contain some cues of a possible future pattern as well? Perhaps the latter prospect, if not likely, is also not unthinkable.

THE PREINDUSTRIAL CITY

In the preindustrial city described by anthropologists, urban space is organized in a fashion completely foreign to our own experience. Unlike the shape we late-twentieth-century Americans have learned to expect for the city—in which the less affluent residents find their housing close to the core of the metropolis, and those of greater means choose the less crowded suburban areas for their residences—the rich in preindustrial cities lived at the core, and the less desirable residential areas clung to the perimeter of the city. Our own American ancestors lived in such "walking cities"—Philadelphia and Charleston—in patterns that were not disturbed until the middle of the nineteenth century.

The preindustrial city is an energy-poor city, a city lacking the energy base to sustain an industrial order. In such a city, economic enterprise centers upon the trade of handcrafted wares in exchange for food, and personal transport is limited to the cart, the carriage, and, in contemporary instances, the bicycle and the overloaded autobus.

Within the energy-poor city, life is limited to what one finds within walking distance, and those options, especially for persons of limited means, are not plentiful. Gideon Sjoberg has described these cities vividly:

> Typically, all or most of the city is girdled by a wall. Inside, various sections of the city are sealed off from one another by walls, leaving little cells, or subcommunities as worlds unto themselves. . . . Minority ethnic groups, especially, may be so sealed off in quarters of their own . . . that they have only tenuous relations with the general populace. As with the gates to the city proper, the entrances to the various walled quarters are secured at night, bringing communication among the units to a halt.
>
> Within the walled precincts congestion is the order of the day. . . . Given the scanty transport media, people reside and work where they have access to the city's special facilities, and because the technology does not allow many multistoried structures, buildings are set closely together, often immediately juxtaposed, to permit a maximum number of people to partake of the advantages of life within the city walls.
>
> The typical street is greatly congested during the day. Here ambulatory vendors hawk their wares, and numerous small shops and stalls front on the street with little or no sidewalk intervening. Indeed, much business is transacted on the street itself. Combine this with the din of children playing, adults gossiping or bargaining, and animals being led to market, and we find life in feudal cities far from placid and uneventful.

Discussing problems of sanitation, refuse disposal, and provision of water in the city, Sjoberg finds each troublesome and inadequately resolved. He comments on specific land use patterns, including: "1) the pre-eminence of the 'central' area over the periphery, especially as portrayed in the distribution of social class; 2) certain finer spatial differences according to ethnic, occupational, and family ties; and 3) the low incidence of functional differentiation in other land use patterns."

Thus, the wealthy live at the center of the city, provided with easy access to the "central governmental and religious structures [that] dominate the urban horizon." Their luxurious dwellings often face inward, "presenting a blank wall to the street—a reflection of the demand for privacy, and the need to minimize ostentation in a city teeming with 'the underprivileged.'"

> The disadvantaged members of the city fan out toward the periphery, with the very poorest and outcastes living in the suburbs, the farthest removed from the center. Houses toward the city's fringes are small,

flimsily constructed, often one-room hovels into which whole families crowd. (Still farther out, well beyond the city limits, are the summer homes or ancillary dwellings of the elite.)

Sjoberg concludes his description of the typical preindustrial city by noting that its "land configuration is in many ways the reverse of that in the highly industrialized communities." Temporally, the pace of life is slow, and most activities are performed in daylight. Populations of between 5,000 and 10,000 predominate, and few cities contain as many as 100,000 persons.

The preindustrial city is not the only energy-short form of spatial organization that is capable of sustaining human existence. Human beings lived for millenia in even simpler societal forms, as hunter-gatherers in rural communities of fewer than 100 persons or in tribal communities of up to several thousands. In these societal forms, in which many millions of persons continue to live today, the nonhuman energy base of society consisted in large part of wood that was gathered or felled and used to cook food and warm small shelters in times of chill. The ability to transport and exchange wood, and then coal, permitted the development of the city in its preindustrial form.

Within the preindustrial cities, a variety of energy industries began to develop. Wood was collected, transported, and sold to urban residents. And, in the 1600s, the mining of coal became organized into an industrial form. Roebuck describes its emergence in Britain: "The greatest demand for coal came from those districts in which wood was becoming scarce. Wood was a raw material with many uses like building houses and making tools and furniture. In relatively densely populated areas, such as around London, the supply was rapidly diminishing; where wood became too precious to burn, the importance of coal grew."

THE INDUSTRIAL TRANSFORMATION

Fueled by the burning of coal in iron boilers, the industrial city took form in the late eighteenth and early nineteenth centuries in Western Europe and the United States. Lewis Mumford writes that the "generating agents of the new city were the mine, the factory, and the railroad." In a dance whose tempo increased dizzyingly, the availability of coal joined with the development of technology to change the face of the U.S. landscape in a few brief decades.

The most fundamental transformation of the shape of the city, however, was introduced by the harnessing of horsepower to a wagon. The horse-drawn streetcar permitted those of greater means to establish their residences on the city's edge and fostered the development of a city modeled on the explosion of wealth to its periphery, rather than its implosion to the core.

The process has been vividly chronicled in Boston by Warner, who notes that the city remained a "walking city" in the 1850s, its diameter the length of an hour's walk — three miles — despite the presence of the omnibus and the steam railroad, two expensive innovations of the preceding quarter-century. The omnibus moved little faster than a walker; the railroad train stopped too infrequently beyond its in-conveniently located central terminal to affect the city's range. But between 1852 and 1873 the horse railroads stretched the "boundary of dense settlement" by ½ mile, and by 1887 by another 1½ miles, "bringing the outer edge of good transportation to four miles from City Hall." By the 1890s, this radius was extended to six miles with the electrification of the street railways. In Philadelphia, the same process saw the exodus of many of the city's wealthier families from their Broad Street mansions to the greener lands of suburban German-town.

The advancement of streetcar technology and the ensuing development of the coal-fired steam engine intensified the decen-tralization of the U.S. city. By the time oil became available for urban transport, and the automobile had been developed to benefit from its availability, the age of "autopia" appeared close to realization. It is that age in which almost all living Americans have been raised; it is also that age that has come to be perceived as increasingly uncertain by an increasing number of American futurists.

The impact of the automobile on the spatial structure of U.S. set-tlements has been as great as its captivity of the life aspirations of Western humankind. To Robert Moses, who shaped the face of the New York metropolis with its interlaced parkway system, the auto was a source of recreation and invigoration for its owners. Those unable to afford a car were to be denied access to the parkway system's green-fringed courses, whose bridges were designed to im-pede the progress of plebian buses. The car came to mean autonomy, potency, and freedom. We built our suburbs and aban-doned our cities for it; we ripped up our streetcar trackage for its boulevards; we invested our riches in an interstate highway net to permit a coast-to-coast drive in forty hours; and we awake in the 1980s to the realization that we now live in a spatial pattern that only the automobile can sustain.

The realization of our national dependency on the automobile has been, in U.S. social criticism, a source for the indulgence of values that sometimes seem a bit effete and precious. Thus for every journalist John Keats, railing against the vacuousness of life behind the wheel, stood a sociologist Scott Greer, remarking on the magnificence of the achievement of Los Angeles and the majestic interlinkage of its metropolis by its net of freeways. And for every writer and conservationist William H. Whyte, Jr., bemoaning the loss of the "last landscape," there were architectural critics Robert Venturi and Denise Scott Brown to write about the aesthetics of the Las Vegas strip. To question our dependence on the automobile in the 1960s and early 1970s was to challenge progress. The automobile fostered what it was that Americans wanted from life: a home on a quiet half-acre, two or three cars to permit mobility for all members of the family, and access to recreational facilities beyond the pale of the creeping megalopolis.

When they thought about the future of our settlement patterns, which was rather infrequently, U.S. urbanists foresaw an extension of the spread patterns that had steadily intensified since 1850 when the horse-drawn streetcar was introduced. For example, writing in 1975 the University of Chicago's Brian Berry proclaimed a future in which "communication is substituted for movement, permitting people to live in an even more spread pattern than they do today. Persons of greater wealth and leisure will find homes and work among the more remote environment of hills, water, and forest, while most will aspire to this as an ideal."

THE ENERGY PROBLEM

And then came the Arab oil embargo of 1973–1974, the natural gas interruptions in the bitter winter of 1977–1978, the gasoline shortages of 1979, the doubling of gasoline prices in 1979–1980, the Iranian oil shutdown of 1979, the rise of inflation to 13 percent in 1980, and the Persian Gulf war of 1980. In short, then came the recognition that affluence, both in its extension and its preservation, had become problematical. We began to look into the future and see the possibility of the hitherto inconceivable: declining standards of living and increasing shortages of energy.

By the 1980 presidential campaign, the problem of energy and growth emerged as a primary national issue, with positions increasingly staked in the soils of divergent political ideologies. On the right, Republican candidate Ronald Reagan called for energy growth by means of the steady development of fossil fuel and nuclear sources, exuding confidence in the eventual development of limitless sources of nuclear energy.

In the center, Democratic nominee Jimmy Carter and independent Republican John Anderson sought to develop a mixed and pragmatic policy rooted in conservation, limited expansion of nuclear research and development, limited growth of fossil fuel extraction, and a visible, if not fully funded, thrust toward the development of renewable sources. As if to signify that the energy issue was primarily one of prudent management, President Carter had named to the position of secretary of energy the former head of a soft-drink corporation, a man more noted for his managerial acumen than his understanding of energy choices.

On the left, Democratic challengers Edward Kennedy and Jerry Brown drifted toward an antinuclear-energy position without fully explaining how energy needs would be met; a new third party, the Citizen's party, nominated as its candidate a widely published advocate of renewable energy, ecologist Barry Commoner. Energy had truly become by 1980 a political issue of the first order.

Surveys and patterns of energy use suggested that attitudes and behaviors regarding energy were shifting (at least among some portions of the population). By 1980, polls consistently showed greater numbers of people giving credence to the reality of a long-term energy problem than denying it. Levels of energy use began to show declines from year to year, especially in gasoline consumption, a phenomenon commonly attributed to a combination of rising prices, declining real income, increased energy efficiency of new automobiles, and the spread of an ethic of conservation. Social scientists found baffling inconsistencies in these patterns of behavioral change; enduring constellations of energy-related attitudes and behaviors were only beginning to congeal at the outset of the 1980s.

The emergence of energy-based ideologies, first in the environmental movements of the 1970s, and then in the national politics of the 1980s, lent definition to three distinct visions of the future of the United States.

These ideologies of energy, as revealed in the 1980 presidential campaign, are those of energy plenitude on the right (enough oil will be found if the price is right, synfuels can be developed, conservation means deprivation), energy pragmatism in the center (both conservation and selective development should be pursued), and energy transformation on the left (small-scale, "appropriate" technology solutions and new conserving lifeways are preferable to continued "hard energy" development). These positions may be arrayed from the optimism and continued faith in progress of the conservative position to the rejection of the belief in continuing technology of the radical left. However, many on the left remain optimistic regarding prospects of developing sufficient renewable energy for the future.

These energy ideologies are largely consistent with the traditions of conservative, liberal, and radical thought, respectively. Conservatives have traditionally voiced their trust in the powers of the free market, backed by a strong national military force and interest. Conservatives have conventionally discounted notions of the "perfectibility of man" in building the good society, and have also, in recent years, been more than willing to bend their faith in the free market to sustain the economic power of struggling corporations. Overall, a faith in the free market, the corporation, and the nation-state sustains the allegiance of conservatives, and they center their energy policy on those forces, in selective combination.

On the left, in contradistinction, the faith has always been strong that individual persons will be able to rise to the challenges of social crisis, if assisted and supported by wise collective political action.

Thus, the marriage of democratic socialism and the appropriate technology movement that is represented by the Citizen's party, and hinted at by Kennedy and Brown, reflects a radical faith in decentralization and individual rationality.

In the center, liberalism and pragmatism—a mixture of left and right—reign. President Carter's critics argued that his "mixture" appeared as multiple and contradictory decisions, but there is no denying the pragmatic intent of his energy policies.

With the election of Ronald Reagan to the presidency, however, an administration was brought to power that based its public ideology on the reaffirmation of U.S. power and plenitude. Reaching into the past for its driving images, the Reagan team reclaimed an energy ideology of bounty and exploitation from Old West days. In asserting this vision, they struck strong chords on a theme of considerable popularity.

IMAGES OF ENERGY PLENITUDE

Of all the tenets of recent American life, none seems more unshakeable than the belief in the infinite availability of energy sources to provide mobility, heating and cooling, and industrial power. We continue to believe that the oil situation is best defined as a temporary aberration in the international pricing structure. We continue to believe that there is no impending exhaustion of oil supplies. And, most optimistically, we continue to believe that some new and plentiful source of energy, perhaps inexhaustible, sits awaiting the next scientific breakthrough for its plentiful employment, ushering in a resolution of all energy problems.

Energy, we love to tell ourselves, is available in nearly infinite quantities. The only problem is to develop new technologies to harness it. Thus, our present problem is seen as one of phasing in these new sources and relying on coal power for the interim period during which oil reserves begin to fail. Dantzig and Saaty drew on a 1971 special issue of *The Scientific American* to fortify their view of the bounty of available energy supplies, as Table 1.1 illustrates:

> Even assuming rates of consumption per capita ten times the average world levels in 1968, man still has truly enormous energy reserves, providing, of course, that scientific techniques can be discovered to tap these sources of energy. It is hoped that in the future methods will be developed for obtaining energy efficiently from fusion and solar radiation.

[Table 1.1]
World Supply of Energy Measured in Years
Before Reserve Sources Are Exhausted,
Assuming Consumption Rates Worldwide Are
Ten Times Current Per Capita Rates

Energy source	Reserve status	Years before exhaustion
Coal, oil, gas	Known reserves	13
	Potential reserves	270
Uranium (U_3O_8)	Accessible known reserves	6
	Accessible potential reserves	6
	Less accessible reserves	10^4
Fusion power	Deuterium from the ocean	3×10^9
Solar radiation	Life of the sun	10×10^9

Source: George B. Dantzig and Thomas L. Saaty, *Compact City: A Plan for a Liveable Urban Environment* (San Francisco: W.H. Freeman, 1973), pp. 129–130. By permission of the authors.

As for the phasing-in problem, William Nordhaus has presented an influential schema for an optimal set of transitions (see Fig. 1.1), assuming the development of breeder reactor viability by the year 2020. Most recently, then-Congressman David A. Stockman,

Republican from Michigan, has argued that proven reserves of fossil fuels have been added more rapidly than consumption so that "nearly five years after the scarcity threat first arose, new reserves are still being added faster than production." Moreover, Stockman asserts that "the planet's accessible natural hydrocarbon reserves readily exceed 20 trillion barrels. This is the equivalent of five centuries of consumption at current rates." Thus, to Stockman, the problem of energy is not one of supply, but rather one of appropriately pricing different energy sources. It is on the assumptions that plentiful fossil fuels remain and that the newer sources of energy can be developed before these fossil fuels are exhausted that confidence in an energy-sufficient future has been maintained.

THE SPECTER OF ENERGY SHORTFALL

Against the voices of energy plenitude, an increasing chorus has suggested the possibility of energy shortfall. Among the most lucid of these voices are those of Denis Hayes who, in his book *Rays of Hope*,

Figure 1.1
Time Path of Optimal U.S. Technological Processes in Solving the Energy Problem, by Demand Categories, 1970–2120 and Beyond

Period	Electricity	Heat — Industrial	Heat — Residential	Transportation — Substitutable	Transportation — Nonsubstitutable
1970-80	Domestic natural gas	Domestic petroleum and natural gas	Imported oil	Domestic and imported oil	
1980-90	Imported liquified natural gas		Imported petroleum		
1990-2000			Imported liquified natural gas		
2000-10	Light-water reactor				
2010-20			Domestic high-cost natural gas	High-cost domestic and imported petroleum	
2020-45		Domestic deep coal	Domestic gasified deep coal, natural gas	Domestic and imported low-cost shale oil and domestic liquified coal	
2045-70			Light-water reactor	Domestic liquified deep coal	
2070-2120		Breeder reactor			Domestic liquified deep coal and high-cost shale oil
2120 to indefinite future					

Source: William Nordhaus, in Robert W. Burchell and David Listokin, *Future Land Use: Energy, Environmental, and Legal Constraints* (New Brunswick, N.J.: Center for Urban Policy Research, 1975), p. 283. By permission of the publisher.

outlines a future in which we shall consider ourselves fortunate to be able to consume as much energy as we do at the present time; Amory Lovins who has written persuasively of the distinction between "hard" and "soft" energy paths; and Barry Commoner whose work often focuses on the politics of energy transformation.

Hayes's argument is based on two major assumptions: first, that up to 80 percent of all available oil and gas supplies are likely to be depleted by the end of the century; and second, that nuclear technology will prove unworkable on a large scale because of intense radioactivity, the problem of disposal of nuclear waste, and the dangers inherent in nuclear war and terrorism. The future of energy, he asserts, lies in renewable energy sources—wind, water, biomass (grain alcohol, methane), and direct sunlight.

Such renewable sources, Hayes contends, could, if assiduously developed, account for up to 75 percent of a modest world energy budget by the year 2025. But they can carry the load only if dramatic savings and reductions in use are implemented, beginning as soon as is possible and feasible.

Lovins describes these renewable sources as "soft" energy paths, in contradistinction to the "hard" paths of fossil fuel and nuclear energy on which we are today so dependent. He defines these soft technologies in terms of five characteristics.

1. They rely on renewable energy flows that are always there whether we use them or not, such as sun and wind on vegetation: or energy income, not on depletible energy capital.
2. They are diverse, so that as a national treasury runs on many small tax contributions, so national energy supply is an aggregate of very many individually modest contributions, each designed for maximum effectiveness in particular circumstances.
3. They are flexible and relatively low technology—which does not mean unsophisticated, but rather easy to understand and use without esoteric skills, accessible rather than arcane.
4. They are matched in scale and in geographic distribution to end-use needs, taking advantage of the free distribution of most natural energy flows.
5. They are matched in energy quality to end-use needs.

The matching of energy sources to the uses to which the energy is put is a crucial aspect of Lovins's thinking. He explains that energy sources are not valued in themselves, as say for their qualities of being electricity or oil, but rather are important for the work they perform for us. Only 8 percent of our current energy uses, he notes, actually requires electricity—which now provides 13 percent of our energy. It is particularly important to use electricity wisely because its production consumes three units of resources (coal or oil) for every unit of usable electricity generated. The two waste units are discharged as heat into the air, and further loss is experienced in the transmission of electricity from its power station to the eventual point of use.

Lovins is fundamentally optimistic about the feasibility of living as well or better than we do now, while consuming substantially fewer energy resources. His vision of continuing energy sufficiency, however, requires the prompt commitment of our national energy systems of production to the paths of soft energy. Whether such a transformation will be achieved in time is a fundamental element of the work of Barry Commoner, scientist and presidential candidate in 1980, who notes that formidable opposition will face the advocates of solar transition.

> The decision to embark at once on the solar transition would mean an unavoidable clash between the national interest and the special interests of the major oil companies and the electrical utilities. In the solar transition, the major oil companies, among the richest and most powerful corporations in the U.S., or the world, would lose their dominant position in the economy. For them, the transition would end the attractive prospect of at least twenty-five more years of escalating energy prices, which—given their rights as private entrepreneurs—would enable them to accumulate huge profits and buy up even larger sectors of the economy.

If the oil companies do not relinquish their hold on the economy, Commoner warns that the solar transition would be "delayed or blocked entirely," though the oil interests "would continue to flourish while the rest of the economy would suffer." Because the rest of industry and the economy as a whole would benefit from solar transition, Commoner observes that "Damage to the private interests of major oil companies seems to be a necessary cost of these larger, social benefits. As economists would say, there is no free lunch."

Commoner concludes his study with substantial, though tempered, optimism:

> It will be difficult, some say impossible, to learn how to merge economic justice with economic progress, and personal freedom with social governance. If we allow the fear of failing in this aim to forestall the effort to achieve it, then failure is certain. But if we firmly embrace

economic democracy as a national goal, as a new standard for political policy, as a vision of the nation's future, it can guide us through the historic passage that is mandated by the energy crisis, and restore to the nation the vitality that is inherent in the richness of its resources and the wisdom of its people.

Earl T. Hayes, formerly the chief scientist at the U.S. Bureau of Mines, summarizes the choices succinctly: "It must be recognized that the United States never had or never will have the petroleum resources to sustain indefinitely the production levels of the last 25 years. In effect, we have been living off our capital all this time and cannot postpone the day of reckoning indefinitely." He concludes: "Energy and gross national product have risen 3 to 3½ percent a year since 1940, and a decrease in the energy growth rate to less than 1 percent a year by 2000 will occasion some fundamental national problems for which we have no precedent. The involuntary conservation brought on by decreased supplies will be exceedingly painful for an unprepared American public."

A PRUDENT WAGER

The purpose of this chapter is not to claim that the Hayes-Commoner-Lovins vision of our energy future is more nearly correct, or more likely to occur, than the conventional *Scientific American*–Nordhaus-Stockman view. Rather, it is to suggest that the alternate vision is sufficiently plausible that a prudent society should consider it when making decisions and recommendations that will involve energy use and conservation for the coming decades and centuries. As Denis Hayes asserts, our options are constrained by long lead time, both for energy transformation and conservation. "Inefficient buildings constructed today will still be wasting energy fifty years from now; oversized cars sold today will still be wasting fuel ten years down the road."

Such prudence may seem perverse to David Stockman, who finds it "evident that the quest for energy has already become a haven for every manner of quack, charlatan, self-aggrandizing economic-interest group, bureaucratic power-seeker, social reformer and intellectually anemic would-be policy-maker that inhabits the American political system." Mr. Stockman might well consider applying his rhetoric to his own argument. Just how reliable has the international market proved to be, even backed by U.S. military might, in restraining the Organization of Petroleum Exporting Countries (OPEC) price rises and the oil supply interruptions occasioned by the Iranian revolution and the war between Iraq and Iran? Mr. Stockman's prescription that "we need do little more than decontrol domestic energy prices, dismantle the energy bureaucracy and allow the U.S. economy to equilibrate at the world level" might well be more helpful as policy analysis if expressed with less dogmatism and inflexibility.

The reality is that our energy future is strewn with pitfalls, each ponderous and none capable of precise determination. It appears wise to base our plans for the future with a consideration in mind of such questions as:

- How long will 500 years' supply of fossil fuels last (at present rate of use)? If use quadruples again over the next quarter-century, and simply doubles that for the following twenty-five years, and again for the next quarter-century, the supply will be exhausted by 2050.
- How much non-U.S. fuel will be made available to us by suppliers, 80 percent of which are located in the lesser-developed countries and 50 percent in the various Communist bloc countries? Perhaps the market will prevail, or perhaps the energy weapon will be used nationalistically, as a moral equivalent of war, to invert a phrase.
- And, finally, what of war itself? How much energy would be consumed in a world war that centered on control of Middle Eastern oil supplies?

Plausible images of both energy plenty and poverty have been developed in great detail, and a number of the most systematic of them are described in Chapter 3. However these images of our energy future vary among themselves, and vary they do—there lurks within almost all of them the recognition that a combination of mismanagement, malevolence, and misfortune might bring us up short on energy supplies, and soon.

At their most frightening, these projections describe an outright shortfall of energy needed to sustain accustomed or anticipated levels of comfort, mobility, and productivity. In his foreword to the present volume, Willis W. Harman asserts that such a future certainly awaits the nonindustrialized world, and the implications of this prediction for the economic and military stability of our own society are immense. Dislike it as we will and deny it as we may, we live in a world in which the risks of nuclear war, total or limited, remain dangerously high. If anything, these risks escalate with every advance of nuclear proliferation and with the increasing recognition of the permanence of underdevelopment for most of the world's citizens and their descendants.

But war is not the only potential harbinger of energy shortfall. So long as we remain heavily dependent upon imported oil, it seems most unlikely that inflation will drop much below the 10 percent mark, and the possibility exists that it might soar well beyond that in the years ahead. Our nuclear future is uncertain at best, and the faith often expressed in fusion energy may possibly remain just that, a faith. The possibility does exist that we may enter an era of scarce and prohibitively expensive oil without developing alternate sources of energy adequate to sustain anything near our present levels of living.

More likely than such a drift toward shortfall is the continuation of present energy trends, in which consumers move with slow but steady force toward reduced use of nonrenewable energy sources and gradually make increased use of the cost-saving benefits of conservation and renewable energy sources. But even in such an apparently incremental process of energy change, the danger remains that the escalation of prices will create severe dislocations in living standards and patterns of distribution. If the price of natural gas is suddenly deregulated, for instance, in all likelihood its price will more than double. And the higher the price of nonrenewable fuel becomes, the greater will be the temptation for those who own the patents and economic capacity to deliver renewable energy to raise their prices to parity with the dwindling nonrenewable sources. One should not discount the willingness nor the ability of energy corporations to act in their own interest in setting prices for their wares that greatly exceed their own production costs, nor should one underestimate their power to restrain the trade of potential competitors who seek to underprice them.

However, if the reader agrees with David Stockman that it is a foolish waste of intellectual and political resources to worry about the possibility that energy shortfall may occur or that energy prices might give rise to vast social dislocations, then there is no need to proceed further with the present volume. But this book will be justified if there is any substantial possibility that either the level of energy availability or pricing will create serious economic or social dislocations in the years ahead.

Ultimately, the choice among views of possible energy futures is a question of faith and skepticism, of seeking to be rational when facing the unknowns of the future. Today's energy choices may, indeed, confront us with a twentieth-century embodiment of Pascal's wager. Writing over 300 years ago, Pascal wrestled with the choice between believing and not believing in God, recognizing that reason could guide him to neither choice, but that a choice was forced since nondecision was in fact a decision not to believe. He presented the choice as a cosmic wager and concluded that the terms of the wager required the choice of belief. "And so our proposition is of infinite force, when there is the finite to stake in a game where there are equal risks of gain and of loss, and the infinite to gain. This is demonstrable; and if men are capable of any truths, this is one."

Is not our choice of an energy future analogous to Pascal's wager? We do not know whether breeder technology will be developed; we do not know how the environment will receive the outpouring of carbon dioxide from the transitional use of coal; we do not know how many of the also unknown oil reserves can be economically recovered. But we do know that world oil and gas consumption cannot quintuple in the coming quarter-century as it did in the last. We do know that the social consequences of an unplanned and precipitous decline in energy availability will be profound and disturbing. We had a glimpse of this process in the winter of 1973–1974 during the oil embargo, and surely it is sobering to reflect on the potential consequences of a more serious and long-term decline in energy on our individualistic, materialistic, and relatively unplanned and undirected social order. George Sternlieb has put it well: "It is my belief that at least short term history as a guide to the future essentially ended in the winter of 1973–74. What we have come to is a scene that has a high potential for being completely underestimated and misread by those who use as a base the history of the last century."

The odds appear to have suddenly shifted on our energy future: shortfall and dislocation appear far more likely than they did scarcely a decade previously. Thus, we might consider shifting our bets in our twentieth-century Pascal's wager to prepare for the possibility of profound energy dislocation in our lives. We would be wise to protect ourselves from the surprise of a possible, if not probable, future. In that way, we can continue to hope for the best, as is conventional, but we can also ready ourselves for the worst. And in energy futures, the worst means being surprised by shortfall. One might well paraphrase Dickens: 75 Quads supplied, 80 needed = Misery; 50 Quads supplied, 45 needed = Happiness.

It now seems prudent to think clearly and plan carefully for a world that may be reshaped by a long-term imbalance between how much energy we harness and how much we believe we need. The following chapters of this book trace some of the consequences that might flow from such an imbalance.

2

Elements of the American Future

The future of any society is unknown in full detail until it emerges, day by day, as the present and then slides into the past. Thinking about the future runs the risks of claiming, on the one hand, to know the unknowable, and of being, on the other hand, too timid to make responsible projections about likely consequences of known trends and possible developments. Despite these risks, the 1970s have seen the gradual, even painful, emergence of futures studies as a reputable field of scholarship. The field has, in the past few years, matured, and its methods and approaches are both more cautious and sophisticated than those of the utopians—Plato, St. Augustine, Sir Thomas More, Edward Bellamy, Aldous Huxley, and George Orwell—whose works make up the main strand of futurism in Western thought. New approaches also seek to avoid the pitfalls of straight-line forecasting and, like many of the utopian theories, do not assume that the future will simply be an extension and magnification of present trends.

The best of contemporary futurist work builds on a sophisticated understanding and analysis of historical and contemporary trends and seeks to extend these trends in the description of patterns of future societal configuration. Among the most prominent contemporary broad-based studies that fully meet these criteria are those of Willis W. Harman and Herman Kahn. Two other studies that brilliantly analyze historical and contemporary trends, but do not fully develop them into future scenarios, are those of Theodore Roszak and Morris Janowitz. A brief consideration of these four approaches will clarify four distinctive approaches to futures study, as developed by practitioners of the art and science of societal study.

Harman and Kahn explicitly accept the academic title of futurist, as their respective recent book titles indicate (Harman's *An Incomplete Guide to the Future;* Kahn's *The Next 200 Years).* Roszak prefers to analyze significant cultural trends in his work (*The Making of the Counterculture, Where the Wasteland Ends,* and *Person/Planet*), while Janowitz explicitly focuses on the recent past in an attempt to identify contemporary societal trends (*The Last Half-Century*).

Both Roszak and Janowitz are dubious of many futurist efforts. Roszak suspects the politics of such futurists as Buckminster Fuller and Alvin Toffler who subscribe to the "belief that the global environment can still be saved by some world-wide system of surveillance, planning, and administration that will finally stabilize world industrialism." Janowitz's skepticism is scientific; to him, futurism is simply not social science. "The efforts of sociologists," he writes, "at global futurology are relatively pointless; even the forecasting of specific statistical time series is a hazardous task."

Kahn, Harman, Roszak, and Janowitz differ among themselves on such issues as the role of advocacy in social science and the most appropriate methodology for the study of the future.

Advocacy and science are generally seen as competing values. Advocacy aims directly to demonstrate the need for societal change while science aims at an "objective" analysis of the directions change might take. Kahn and Barry Bruce-Briggs have described this distinction well:

> It may be impossible to completely separate descriptive and normative futurology; nevertheless, we feel it is extremely important and rewarding to make a serious attempt. Unfortunately, the field of future studies is thick with normative forecasting masquerading as descriptive. Many prognostications of many distinguished American thinkers are statements of what the author wants to happen, not necessarily what he thinks will happen, and frequently they are a bald pitch for some express policy or program. If done openly and honestly this is a perfectly valid method of political advocacy, with many honorable precedents (such as Bellamy's *Looking Backward*), but it tells us very little about what the future will be, except insofar as it is influenced by the ideas and desires of important men today.

Roszak is one who adopts the advocacy style. His interest is less in predicting the future than in constructing a future in which the values he espouses will be able to thrive and prosper. His style is to warn of the potency of prevailing trends and to leave open a ray of hope that a better choice, however unlikely, will be chosen by persons who see the wisdom of his position. Kahn, Harman, and Janowitz all seek to make both scientific and advocacy statements, but to separate them more explicitly. Thus, Harman identifies a movement toward "transindustrial society" that "seems both to be underway and to be desirable," while Kahn identifies four images of "earth-centered perspective," and notes that he is "generally optimistic" about the problems raised by the more pessimistic views. Unlike Roszak, who identifies industrialism as the enemy of human progress, Kahn contends that "the effort to achieve a postindustrial society is on balance a worthwhile one; and further, that priorities which emphasize technological advancement and economic growth, but with prudence and care, are likely to be acceptable and largely beneficial."

Janowitz divides his analysis between the "contemplative" approach of description of trends and the "manipulative" approach of viewing problems through the perspectives of processes as seen by leaders. The second perspective allows him to offer comments on ways in which sufficient "social control" can be maintained in American society. Janowitz adopts the academic stance of commentator: "I prefer to believe that the contribution of social scientists to societal changes must be indirect and must emphasize clarification more than direct political leadership and action."

Methodologies of future study differ as well. Kahn and Harman develop a single scenario that they perceive as most plausible, challenging the reader to develop alternative constructions. Roszak focuses on problems and does not develop specific scenarios, and Janowitz eschews explicit prediction. All four, however, share a commitment to the analysis of societal development as a process that systematically integrates social, cultural, economic, and political forces. And each provides a wealth of analytical grist for the student of the future, as well as a honed perspective on both what *will likely be* and what *might best be* the future of Western society.

The futurism of this work seeks to borrow Kahn's ability to see alternatives (even if unpleasant), Harman's belief that societal transformation can be profound, Roszak's passion that choices need to be articulated, and Janowitz's assertion that there is much to be learned from the past.

SOME POSSIBLE ENERGY FUTURES

Let us begin our examination of U.S. futures by considering four ways in which our energy future might develop over the next several decades. It is possible that events will unfold this way:

1. A relatively smooth transition is made from the oil-based energy dependence of the twentieth century to the coal, nuclear, and renewable bases of the twenty-first century.

Although prices rise rapidly for oil and gas, consumption of these fuels drops rapidly as they become replaced by a combination of fuels in more ample supply. Despite the fears of critics and skeptics, nuclear energy, in its breeder and fusion forms, is safely harnessed for the production of electric power; coal is increasingly used in place of oil for electric generation, as well; and a wide variety of renewable fuels are developed, at reasonable cost, to perform many needed services in home heating and cooling and, to lesser extent, in the powering of moving vehicles.

Overall, only 30 percent more energy is needed in the year 2000 than in 1980, but it accomplishes far more work, as end-use is more rationally paired to power source. Additionally, the widespread acceptance of the principle that "conservation means more money in your wallet" leads to dramatic reductions in the amount of energy needed for home heating and cooling as well as for personal transport. By the year 2000, the energy crisis has become history.

It is also possible that our energy future over the next twenty years might develop this way:

2. The determination of the Reagan, Bush, and Stockman administrations to create a free market for energy development and sales (except for nuclear energy, which remains highly subsidized by government), yields only modest increments in energy supplies. Energy prices rise rapidly, contributing to a lowering of living standards of almost all Americans below the median income. Those who can afford the more expensive and effective means of conservation and renewable energy use do so, but these innovations trickle down to lower income groups very slowly. As a burgeoning market for solar energy develops, it is captured by large oil companies diversifying their energy holdings, and prices of all forms of energy remain high.

The promise of nuclear development remains largely unfulfilled. While the breeder reactor is widely employed, fusion energy is not brought into effective use. Coal becomes the principal fuel in the United States, but its production increments barely keep pace with the decline in oil production. The United States remains dependent upon overseas sources for one-third of its oil. As the twenty-first century opens, the need to resolve the growing energy crisis is paramount on the national agenda.

It is not beyond the realm of possibility that our energy future might take this form:

3. Despite a national commitment to the rapid exploitation of remaining nonrenewable fuels–by price deregulation, reductions of standards of environmental degradation, development of shale and coal sources, and continuing nuclear development–widespread shortages of affordable energy characterize the 1990s. Following several disastrous nuclear accidents, both breeder and fusion efforts are abandoned commercially, and the remaining reactors on line are shut down permanently. Oil imports are denied to the United States by the treaty with the 117 victorious nations that concludes the Persian Gulf war of 1987, ending the conflict that produced the nuclear destruction of Los Angeles, Philadelphia, Leningrad, and Tehran.

    In the wake of the decline in oil and nuclear supply, a crash program is developed to expand coal production, increase solar collection, and reduce energy use by conservation. Such an effort fails to avert the widespread dislocations in society and economy of a massive energy shortfall, and it takes until the year 2000 to stabilize energy production and use at pre–World War II levels. Nearly every family experiences substantial declines in living standards, levels of comfort, and access to personal mobility. In the year 2000, as rioters seize control of corporate headquarters buildings in seventeen cities, martial law is declared. National leadership calls for a decade of sacrifice to achieve energy sufficiency through self-help.

There may even be just the slightest chance that the following might happen:

4. Following the resounding Democratic victory in 1984, President Mondale and Secretary of Energy Denis Hayes commit their administration to a vigorous program of conservation, renewable-resource development, expansion of coal mining, and phasing out of nuclear energy. Levels of energy use in 1980 are thereby sustained throughout the decade, while

standards of living increase as the benefits of conservation are achieved. Despite the approaching exhaustion of many energy sources on a worldwide level, the United States achieves energy independence by the year 2000 and appears to have assured its energy sufficiency into the decades and centuries beyond.

These four images vary both in their optimism and the likelihood that they will come to pass. They are, of course, not the only images of our energy future that may be constructed. The situation is sufficiently fluid (or perhaps insufficiently so) that many other futures may plausibly be constructed. These images are presented as representations of plausible lines of development, and the reader is invited to modify them as seems useful.

Of the four futures just presented, the first and the last tend to be optimistic, the third painful if not outright disastrous, and the second somewhat middling. Thus, the first and the last may be considered "Good Luck" futures, in which events are touched with good fortune and we receive the benefits of a series of wise choices and lucky breaks that turn the future toward a happy outcome. The third may be seen as a "Hard Luck" future, in which we fall victim to a series of poor policy choices and bad breaks that present us with a gloomy, if not tragic, set of predicaments. The second may be seen as the "Continuity" scenario, in which the future remains much like the recent past.

THE STRUCTURE OF THE FUTURE

Futures unfold as the ever-changing outcomes of billions of individual decisions and actions. These individual behaviors are channeled through major societal institutions. Thus, each of us participates, whether willingly or not, in a national economy and culture.

Four institutional sectors are particularly important and may be seen as basic elements of our future. These institutions perform the basic tasks required for societal development. Sociologist Talcott Parsons has identified these tasks as adaptation, goal-attainment, integration, and latent pattern-maintenance.

Parsons explained that the problem of adaptation, of securing the economic resources needed to establish the basis of societal existence, is assigned to the economy. The problem of goal-attainment, of achieving the ends deemed crucial for societal development, is the

task of the polity. The third task, integration, involves linking dis-
parate social groups and is the focus of the voluntary sector. The final
task, latent pattern-maintenance, is that of achieving meaning and
coherence, and it is the work of the cultural institutions of church,
school, and family.

In this chapter, the elements of these four institutional factors will
be discussed, and several images of their future development will be
suggested. The images will take the form of the Continuity, Good
Luck, and Hard Luck scenarios.

In Chapter 3, the factors will be combined into several scenarios for
the future of the United States. These scenarios, in turn, set the stage
for the rest of the analysis. If we conclude that our future is fundamentally a bright and resource-rich one, most of the considerations of spatial implications of energy shortfall will prove to be un-
necessarily pessimistic. If, on the other hand, we conclude that there
is a significant chance that our future will be touched by the gloomier
sides of the factors, it will surely prove prudent to attend to the
analysis of the remaining chapters.

So, what then of possible futures in our economic, cultural,
associational, and governmental life? Let us explore their elements
and hazard predictions of three possible futures for each.

THE U.S. ECONOMY: GROWTH OR MELTDOWN?

The role of the economy in society is to produce and allocate
goods and services that are deemed necessary and desirable. The
U.S. economy in the 1980s is deeply troubled by problems of inflation, unemployment, corporate domination, and distribution. A
discussion of these problems leads to the development of our
economic scenarios.

Inflation

That the endemic inflation of prices beyond accustomed rates of income growth has become the primary problem of Americans is
dificult to dispute. Inflation was the central issue of the 1980
presidential campaign, and like the weather, inflation beyond
growth, or "stagflation," has become a national preoccupation.

Economists as well have joined in the orgy of complaint, and their
explanations of inflation's causes are as diverse as the range of
citizens' explanations. Some economists claim that the bloating of
monetary supply is to blame. Others assert that it is the lack of control
on incomes that fuels our current inflation. Yet others see the shock

of "exogenous factors" like the OPEC price rises as the basic cause.

From the right comes the assertion that only the taking of the full medicine of the business cycle, and the bearing of its required recession, without counter-cyclical government spending, will lead to a reduction in inflation. From the left comes the contention that capitalism itself has become inflationary, with a highly bureaucratized "planning system" that has successfully insulated itself from the worst ravages of inflation and the loss of productivity.

The danger of the situation is captured by William Safire's observation that "our economic engine is in a state of meltdown." Edward Cornish echoes this fear by noting that the combination of lack of liquidity, heavy real estate speculation, threats to the automobile, rising energy prices, high cost of labor and capital, and financial disorder may trigger a depression in the 1980s that will be more severe than that of the 1930s.

Perhaps the clearest and most measured analysis of the future of U.S. inflation is that presented by the Joint Economic Committee of Congress in 1979.

The committee explains inflation in terms of three sets of causes:

1. Government monetary and fiscal policies;
2. Exogenous factors, such as OPEC oil pricing, that contribute to a "shock rate" of inflation;
3. Inflationary expectations, which affect unit labor costs.

Three scenarios are developed by the committee: "baseline," "optimistic," and "pessimistic." Of central concern to the committee is the need to reverse declining rates of productivity that plagued our economy in the late 1970s. Assuming this reversal can be achieved, the committee sees growth in the Gross National Product (GNP) between 2.7 percent and 3.6 percent between 1980 and 1984 in its pessimistic and baseline scenarios, and the range widens to 1.5 percent and 5.1 percent between 1985 and 1989.

In the committee's pessimistic scenario, inflation is seen to average close to 10 percent, while in the baseline scenario, it drops below 6 percent by 1989. If inflation rises at close to 10 percent per year throughout the decade, the cumulative rise in prices will exceed 140 percent. Thus, the pensioner's $10,000 in 1980 will barely purchase $4,000 worth of goods and services by decade's end, and a salary of $50,000 will be required to meet the expenses paid by a $21,000 income at present.

When it is recognized that the committee's baseline model rests on assumptions of reversal of productivity slowdown, no interruptions in energy supply, GNP growth at historic levels, only moderate rises in food prices, and fairly rapid rises in exports, even the baseline model clearly is seen to be highly optimistic in its expectations. More realistic would appear to be the committee's pessimistic scenario, based on no growth in oil consumption, oil price rises 20 percent above inflation, and one or more interruptions in oil supply. Even these assumptions may prove optimistic in light of the near-doubling of oil prices in 1979, and the continuing demonstration of the uncertainty of receipt of Iranian, Iraqi, and Saudi oil supplies by the United States. Leonard Silk has noted that "growth in output-per-worker averaged 3 percent through most of American history. In the 1980s, it seems likely to average 1 or 2 percent." His prognosis lends support to the committee's pessimistic scenario: low growth, high inflation, and little or no growth in real personal income.

Unemployment

The 1980s will also be troubled by problems of inadequate levels of employment. It appears likely that a substantial surplus of workers to jobs will characterize the decade. Further, an increasing number of workers will be "overqualified" for the positions they hold and will view themselves as both underpaid and underutilized.

Trends producing these problematic outcomes include—

- The elimination of many entry-level jobs to automation. Martin Ernst of Arthur D. Little, Inc., predicts, "automation of the service industries will cut out starting jobs for the relatively untrained—people stamping prices in supermarkets, bank tellers, and processors. They'll go the way of the elevator operator."
- Continuing pressure on the job market provided by the return to work by women. Leonard Silk writes, "more women than ever will seek jobs, partly to combat the effects of chronic inflation."
- A decline in the number of workers choosing early retirement—an outcome of both the extension of the age of mandatory retirement to seventy years and inflation. Economist Eli Ginzburg has remarked, "Early retirement? If this inflation keeps up, nobody will be able to get out early."
- Continuing entry of migrants from the Far East and, especially, Mexico. Jerome Rosow, director of Work in America Institute, explains that our need for Mexican oil and gas will make it impossible to close our Mexican border. "We will be repeating

the experience of the European immigration of the
1920s. . . . And Mexico's population could double by the
end of the century."

The effect of these trends will include a significant heightening of
competition in the workplace—at the point of initial hire, for promo-
tion, and for tenure. Harvard economist Richard B. Freeman sees
"fierce competition for promotions, coupled with substantial career
disappointment for many," with the corollary that many workers will
be forced to content themselves "with especially low income for their
entire lives."

Leonard Silk, in his brilliant rendition of the pessimistic economic
scenario for the 1980s, notes that social tensions will increase not
only between the sexes but also between the classes.

> Unionized workers will increase their relative advantage in income
> over non-unionized professionals. A surplus of humanities and social
> science college graduates may come to form an "upper proletariat,"
> providing a source of growing social and political embitterment, as they
> did in post–World War I Europe.
>   Embitterment could extend down the work scale as well. In an
> economy growing too slowly, labor is likely to step up its resistance to
> technological change and its insistence on job security, and manage-
> ment is likely to try harder to keep out or get rid of unions, both to hold
> down costs and to make organizational changes. In many offices and
> factories, smart machines may be regarded as more desirable than
> human machines.

Economist Arnold Weber concurs with this judgment: "The next
decade will be a time of increased tension and potential conflict
among the various groups in the labor force." And all of this unfolds
in a nation whose pool of officially unemployed workers was headed
toward 9 million in 1981 and whose "discouraged" work force, not
actively looking for work but potentially employable, amounts to
perhaps twice that number.

Both Janowitz and Roszak note that worker dissatisfaction is
already high in contemporary U.S. factories and corporations,
though Janowitz recalls Robert Blauner's discovery that "the more
complex the machinery and the more individual responsibility and
variation the technology produces and permits, the greater the
satisfaction." Roszak, more pessimistic, finds work within the
"coddled" white-collar corporate world almost as "exploitive and

humiliating" as the work he once performed in a dismal chromeplating plant.

Three bright spots mark this otherwise gloomy set of trends. First, the increase in the proportion of working women will likely give rise to increased patterns of flexible work hours and increasing calls for the humanization of work. Second, the reduction by decade's end in the number of youths seeking access to the labor market may relieve some pressure on rates of unemployment and underemployment. And, third, the rate of new job creation, estimated at 1.3 million annually between 1980 and 1985 by Arnold Weber, will provide employment for many who enter the job market in the years ahead.

Corporate Control

It is a truism of the late-twentieth-century world that we live in the age of the corporation. Domestically, half our economic assets are owned by the 1,000 largest corporations. Internationally, many of these corporations are multinational in their scope and wield powers that exceed those of many nation states.

Many employed in our large corporate institutions, whether they be conglomerates, universities, or even manufacturing establishments, have come to enjoy an unparalleled level of job security and compensation, especially at the professional and management levels. Cost-of-living adjustments to wages soften the impact of inflation on these employees, and seniority and tenure provisions provide for the certainty of continued employment.

The corporation has repealed the application to itself of many provisions of free-enterprise economics and has won protection against economic failure by the presumption that it will be shored up by governmental assistance when bankruptcy threatens, as the Lockheed Corporation demonstrated in the 1970s and the Chrysler Corporation demonstrated in the early 1980s.

Increasingly, corporate leaders attend to mandates of "corporate social responsibility," although it remains unclear to what degree this phrase implies more than a subtle marketing of corporate interest in the guise of wider concerns. As Gordon Schochet has noted: "When the business community regularly responds to society's demands for responsible behavior as one of its ordinary functions, it will begin to see itself as an integral part of society rather than as a separate institution with its own interests. But until these changes occur, business is likely to find itself resented, attacked, regulated, and restricted."

Beyond the corporate or "planning," system lies a rudimentary "capitalist" system, in which as many as 12 million small firms and individual entrepreneurs compete for the residual 50 percent of the economic pie. Those in this sector are protected only by welfare, food stamps, and unemployment insurance, if they are eligible, to sustain them in hard times. Here are located many members of such social categories as young people, women, and minority group members. Ours has become an age of "positional status," and the key to economic security is a post within the great corporate institutions that dominate the U.S. and world economy.

Distribution

The fourth and final aspect of the economy to be considered here is the pattern of distribution of the rewards of economic life. These rewards consist primarily of wealth and income.

Wealth and income are distributed along quite different lines. The lion's share of wealth is owned by a small minority of the population. Most Americans own little more than their car, their personal possessions, and their homes. The top 20 percent of American families, however, control almost 80 percent of our national wealth. There has been little shift throughout this century in that pattern.

Income, on the other hand, is more widely distributed than wealth. The top 20 percent controls 44 percent of income. Further, the income share received by the bottom 40 percent has increased between 1929 and the present. This group received 12.5 percent of total income at the onset of the Depression; by 1977 its share had grown to 14.6 percent. When transfer income from government programs of cash support is added, the share of the bottom 40 percent rises to 17.3 percent.

It is most unlikely that our historic tendency toward decreasing economic inequality will be sustained in the years ahead. As Lester Thurow has argued, the entrance into the labor force of large numbers of middle-class women, most of whom are or will be married to middle-class men, is sufficient to reduce the income shares of the bottom 60 percent. The adoption of the Reagan administration's program of "economic recovery," with its massive transfers of income and program support from the bottom 60 percent to the top 1 percent, further assures a "counter-distribution" of income in the coming decade.

What is true for income may even more strongly apply to wealth. Its sheltering from taxation may well become more assured, and the numbers of those with negative wealth (debts exceeding assets) may increase.

ECONOMIC FUTURES

When the overall development of the U.S. economy in the years ahead is assessed, the factors of inflation, employment, corporate control, and distribution must be considered. Their interaction gives rise to a myriad of economic futures, three of which are now presented.

A Continuity Future

Inflation remains substantially above historic levels in the United States (close to 10 percent) and reflects the approaching exhaustion of many vital resources and a persisting stagnation of economic productivity. Real per capita income continues to decline for almost all employees outside the corporate sector and for some within it.

The 1980s are characterized by a crisis in employment, with unemployment rates running at recessionary levels as job expansion fails to keep up with the entry of "baby-boom" children into the labor force through mid-decade. Unemployment rates approach 10 percent, and the proportion of discouraged workers increases to 30 percent. Automation, while it permits increasing numbers of professionals to work from home at their personal computer stations, continues to reduce the number of jobs available, especially in industry, just as the number of persons seeking work expands to record levels. Anxiety increases among manual workers, the retired, and the underemployed.

By the 1990s a number of new trends reduces unemployment rates: Job sharing is established as a result of the women's movement and the high female unemployment of the 1980s, the development of solar energy in decentralized communities opens many new jobs in quasi-agricultural work, and fewer new entrants seek access to work.

Concentration of economic assets remains in the hands of the Fortune 500 corporations, and mergers within this sector lead to even greater concentration among the largest of these conglomerates. This concentration is accompanied by increased governmental interest in corporate practice, profits, and governance, such that some perceive the economy as "partially socialized" by the year 2000. Others, however, see the control running in the other direction, with corporate elites increasingly represented in top governmental positions.

Outside the "planning sector," a rudimentary capitalist economy continues to function, the source of livelihood for the underemployed, most minorities, and many under thirty-five years of age. These persons compete for economic survival in a "hidden economy" beyond the tax collector, and in a variety of service, "new entrepreneurial," and "appropriate" technology enterprises.

Within the corporation, concern for the productivity and satisfaction of a work force effectively tenured by labor-management bargaining leads to a burgeoning of internal welfare programs: social services for employees and their families, recreational activities, and volunteerism programs, among them. Corporate managers seek to establish a sense of community with their employees, without sharing with them the actual prerogatives and responsibilities of corporate governance, which some workers and unions demand with increased insistence. "Corporate social responsibility" remains a phrase without clarity or substance.

The year 2000 is reached with 10 percent of the population remaining in poverty, and another 25 percent just above the poverty line. The distribution of wealth and income has become somewhat more unequal than it was at the beginning of the 1970s.

Consumers have long since learned to adjust to the slow erosion of their income by continuing "stagflation." The economy remains an ungainly, though relatively steady, source of slow and unequal growth.

A Good Luck Future

Owing to a slowing in OPEC price rises and the preservation of an uninterrupted flow of imported oil, a reversal of declining productivity, and effective governmental control of the wage-price spiral, inflation rates fall below 6 percent by 1986 and remain below that level through the year 2000. Real disposable income rises at 3.5 percent per year, and the unemployment rate is reduced to 3.5 percent by 1990. Despite pessimistic forecasts, the 1980s prove to be about as favorable as the early 1970s and far happier than the late 1970s. This favorable development carries through the 1990s.

Control over the rate of inflation reduces pressure on some men, particularly those approaching seventy years of age, and on women to enter the labor market. Alternatives in family structure make legitimate the temporary role of "house-husband," and developments in volunteerism allow other nonemployed adults to view themselves and their contributions positively. Early retirement remains possible as pensions become more adequate and are not drastically eroded by inflation. The United States avoids the crisis in work availability that seemed almost inevitable at the beginning of the decade.

The corporation retains its centrality in U.S. economic activity, but it also becomes a community for its workers who participate in its control. Experiments in employee decision-making prove constructive and lead to some pilot programs in employee management and ownership. As the corporation becomes increasingly characterized by democratic process and governance, new and vital conceptions and programs of social responsibility are developed.

The year 2000 is reached with the ranks of the poor virtually emptied by the steady march of economic progress. Not only is poverty nearly eliminated, but also a modest redistribution of income and wealth to the favor of lower-income persons characterizes the 1980s and 1990s.

Consumers count on small but steady increments in their purchasing power. The mature U.S. economy enters the twenty-first century as a machine of continuing flexibility and power.

A Hard Luck Future

Fed by what by 1983 is widely known as "Reagan's folly," inflation soars unchecked through the 1980s, reaching 15 percent by 1983, and 25 percent by 1984. Supply-side economics is abandoned by Republicans and Democrats alike in 1984, but the landslide Democratic victory that year does not retard the explosion in the rate of inflation, which reaches 50 percent by 1990. Simultaneously, the spread of worldwide depression threatens all national economies as the fifty-year "Kondratieff cycle" takes firm hold. After a period of substantial social chaos and conflict, currency is reissued in 1991, and a strictly controlled economic order is centrally established.

Unemployment reaches depression levels, giving rise to a permanent minority of disaffected and untrained nonparticipants in the work force. These individuals provide many recruits for the ranks of professional crime, social disorder, and permanent dependency.

Tensions between the corporate sector and the rudimentary market sector increase as the competition for positional status in the planning sector gives rise to fierce individual and group competition. Increasingly, political and consumer organizations identify the corporation as the cause of social dissatisfaction and inequality and mount a telling political movement aimed at its breakup. Socioeconomic conflict mounts, and state force is increasingly used to forestall the perceived threat of revolution.

The year 2000 is reached with the ranks of the poor swelled to 25 percent. Another 30 percent of the population subsists on an income below 150 percent of the poverty line, which is set at $80,000 per year in 1990, the equivalent of $8,400 in 1981. A small wealthy minority grows richer, but the middle-class life styles of the early 1980s have all but disappeared by the outset of the terrifying 1990s. The economy experiences its "meltdown," and its restructuring proceeds from a base of discouragement and devastation.

U.S. CULTURE: PRIVATISM OR TRANSFORMATION?

The 1970s will likely be known to future historians by Tom Wolfe's phrase "the Me Decade"—an era of divorce, self-improvement, and consumer debt. Apt as this identification of the 1970s' redirection from the "turbulent 1960s" may appear to be, a more recent development, born of the inflation of the late 1970s, may prove even more significant. If 1979 proves to be the turning point in U.S. affluence—the peak year for material wealth for most Americans in our history—the 1980s will be the first in a long series of decades in which coping with declining living standards will be a central theme. Leonard Silk notes that while personal income will continue to grow, inflation will soak up most of its gains. Moreover, "the rise in the cost of energy relative to the prices of other goods and services may make people feel less able to afford both the luxuries and some of the necessities of life."

Values

Willis Harman calls the contemporary era a time of transformation, in which the very paradigm of our industrial era (production, scientific method, faith in material progress, and pragmatic values) becomes lost. He views the industrial-era paradigm as failing in five central ways:

1. It fails to provide each individual with an opportunity to contribute to the society and to be affirmed by it in return.
2. It fails to foster more equitable distribution of power and justice.
3. It fails to foster socially responsible management of the development and application of technology.
4. It fails to provide goals that will enlist the deepest loyalties and commitments of the nation's citizens.
5. It fails to develop and maintain the habitability of the planet.

Harman sees the emergence, in the 1980s, of a "transindustrial" paradigm with the following characteristics:

1. It will perceive the rootedness of dilemmas of industrial society in the values of the previous paradigm.
2. It will recognize that scientific explanations and religious metaphors need not be contradictory.
3. It will assume the existence of a testable spiritual order.
4. It will embody an ecological ethic of concern for the whole.
5. It will involve a teleological view of life and evolution, extending the scientific world view into the domains of hitherto authoritarian religion.

Daniel Yankelovich has done the most systematic research on the emerging shape of the American culture. He concludes that an "embryonic ethic" is developing in the 1980s. This ethic centers "around two kinds of commitment: forming closer and deeper personal relationships, and trading some instrumental values for sacred/expressive ones."

The quest for relationships is illustrated by an increased search for community, a focus on openness and honesty in family relationships, and a renewed commitment to long-term marital stability. The search for sacred and expressive values is reflected by the development of "reverential thinking" in the areas of religion, patriotism, and community.

Yankelovich's embryonic ethic, as documented by emergent trends in survey data, is what Marilyn Ferguson has called the "aquarian conspiracy," Alvin Toffler "the third wave," and Willis Harman "transindustrial transformation." It is a process of cultural change that involves shifts in individual life ways that occur independently, or even in spite of, governmental policy, corporate advertisement, or social-movement advocacy. It is a way of experiencing the world and how to make meaning of it, and is an intensely personal process of development.

Demography and Life Style

Values themselves are often shaped by changing demographic patterns, though few types of predictions are more uncertain than those that seek to determine future birth rates and the kinds of life styles people will want and choose. In a careful analysis, Harleigh Trecker provides as full a set of predictions as are warranted by the uncertainties in these areas. He notes that, although the "population bomb" is not likely to explode, population gains are likely at both the oldest and youngest ends of the population scale, as birth rates make a modest recovery from their late 1970s trough and members of the 1940s baby-boom cohort move into their sixties following the turn of the century. Women will continue to outlive and thereby out-number men; minority population will continue to grow at a more rapid rate than white population; and Western and Southern states will continue to experience more rapid growth than Eastern and Midwestern states.

The difficulty of foreseeing future life styles is exemplified by two further predictions of Trecker's. First, he asserts that the goal of family stability will be countered by the continuing impact of marital in-stability on the nuclear family. Silk reinforces the point by noting that "the trend is already evident; in 1978, there were a little over two million marriages, and a little over one million divorces."

This trend might not continue long into the future, however. It is possible, for instance, that the pressure of declining real income will prevent many husbands and wives from choosing divorce. Husbands may be restrained by the increasing difficulty of maintaining their own single's needs for housing and sustenance along with their con-tinuing support of children, whatever the future of alimony. Wives, on the other hand, may take increasingly into account the enormous representation of divorced women among the poor and near-poor and choose to retain a poor marriage against the uncertainties of in-dependence.

A second prediction of Trecker's may also be redirected. He notes that the goal of home-ownership will be countered by the reality of ever-higher housing prices and the persistence of slums. Silk again agrees: "The rapidly growing number of households will keep pressure on housing. By the end of the 1980s, 45 percent will be headed by single people."

This prediction may be deflected by a slowing in the divorce rate; it also neglects the tendency of individuals and families to form new household units in times of economic distress. Thus, many singles continue to purchase homes, sometimes with other co-owning singles. Many young adult family members move back into their parents' homes, reducing the rate of single-person households. Any slowing in the divorce rate will reduce pressure for new housing. Finally, an end to the real estate boom would lead to a leveling, or even a decline, in house prices, though probably not to any fall in mortgage interest rates.

The Information Revolution

Another prediction of Trecker's seems less likely to be countered. He notes that developments in telecommunications will permit us to conduct an increasing proportion of our business, domestic, and recreational activities at home. Molitor has put it well:

> A wide range of new and emerging information technologies will reshape many facets of society. Some of these innovations will mean drastic changes for the transportation industry. Americans are not far away from the time when people will conduct many of their transactions—banking, shopping, and even jobs—electronically. People will no longer have to commute to work, but will communicate instead. High energy costs will encourage the rapid introduction of elaborate electronic home entertainment systems.
>
> The information revolution promises a vast new range of potential home information services—electronic fund transfer systems, electronic shopping, electronic mail terminals, interactive TV, pay cable TV, teleconferencing, video recorders, and home computers.

The possibility of an increasingly home-based life style, enabled by telecommunications and constrained by scarcity, suggests that the family will both retain its viability and be subject to increasing and prolonged stresses. Some of these pressures may be absorbed by strengthened neighborhood-based systems of interpersonal activity, cooperative problem-solving, and recreation. It is possible that the 1980s may see a modest rebirth of local community life in the United States, but it is also possible that we may experience an increased level of domestic frustration and violence.

CULTURAL FUTURES

The way in which the forces of privatism and transformation are played out in the years ahead will have a decided impact on the way we shall live. Three possible futures are described.

A Continuity Future

The 1980s experience a titanic struggle between two forces of values: the self-centered, materialistic force of the "me generation" and the other-centered, meaning-questing force of an ethic of ecological and self-realization. Out of this struggle emerge new systems of meaning, both religious and scientific. Many new paths are proposed as making sense of the cosmos and bringing individuals into closer touch with the manifold dimensions of reality. Both new humanist and fundamentalist religions receive increased numbers of participants. Some of these efforts give rise to the collective hysteria of cult movements, religious hucksterism, and efforts to impose puritan values and behaviors upon an unwilling majority.

Continuing demographic transition receives the careful attention of policymakers. Mini baby-booms develop as the postwar "baby-boomers" reach their late twenties and early to mid-thirties in the 1980s and produce a baby boomlet of their own. The absolute number and proportion of seniors rise, the security of their retirement seriously threatened by inflation. Snowbelt population continues to decline. Sunbelt population increases, but not at precipitous levels, owing to the adoption of population control ordinances throughout the Sunbelt and the automobile-dependence of most Western and Southwestern metropolitan structures.

Life styles are characterized by a continuing search for locality-based community. Neighborhood self-help, both formal and informal, greatly expands; experimental life styles are developed in quasi-rural communes aimed at living in voluntary simplicity.

A Good Luck Future

The majority of Americans come gradually to accept a set of "new-age" values adapted to life in the twenty-first century. Resource conservation is accepted as a way of life. Quality of life remains a central goal, but increasingly is realized in interactive communities on a local scale. Active participation thus becomes widespread in cultural and social life, while telecommunications permit home-based access to a hitherto unreachable variety of cultural entertainments.

The threat of authoritarian cults and movements to individual and group liberty is decisively repulsed. By 1990, the antiabortion movement, the Moral Majority, and the Senate Subcommittee on National Security have receded into the obscurity of history.

The "edges" of demographic transition prove to be somewhat smoother than anticipated. Social Security keeps pace with inflation, and retirees maintain income security.

A Hard Luck Future

The forces of self-centeredness, materialism, and privatism that characterized the 1970s intensify, unrestrained by traditions of religion, volunteerism, or social responsibility. The welfare state is steadily dismantled by forces of tax revolt. Economic and political life becomes characterized by "tooth-and-claw" competition and conflict. Cult activity thrives and extends beyond religion into political and economic life. Abortion is outlawed; school prayer is required; the public school systems of twenty-three large cities close with the extension of school vouchers; and loyalty checks lead to the dismissal of 15 percent of the public work force.

The "aging" of the United States requires a 50 percent cutback in Social Security benefits and threatens the harmony of relations between elders and their juniors. A desperate rush to the Sunbelt exacerbates economic dislocation and yields few settled lives for the new migrants.

THE U.S. POLITY: IN WHOSE INTEREST?

Few forms of human endeavor are subject to as wide a set of interpretations as politics. From one perspective, politics is an ennobling human endeavor, in which citizens transcend themselves in the processes of collective policy choice and development. To others, politics is a dirty game in which self-interest is advanced by the shameless sale of the public trust. Two main aspects of our political life are explored in this section: governance and empowerment.

Governance

The coming decades give promise of change in our governing structures, particularly in the ways our political parties function. The direction of these shifts has been charted by political scientist Thomas Wm. Madron, who has studied the predictions of forty prominent political scientists regarding the U.S. political future.

Noting that the period from 1960 to 1976 saw two dramatic trends in voting behavior—one the decline in exercise of the ballot, the other away from identification as either Republican or Democrat—Madron and his panel of political scientists find that both these trends are expected to carry into the 1980s.

Among the trends expected in the 1980s are:

- Increased issue- and candidate-orientation of voters
- Decline of political parties in importance and influence
- Rise of antiparty ideology, which centers on election of nonaffiliated candidates

The following trends have a probability of greater than one in three.

- Permanent decline in voter turnout for presidential elections
- Precipitous decline in the number of volunteer workers in both major parties
- Permanent schism in the Republican party, with the liberal faction leaving or being expelled

Morris Janowitz seconds Madron's predictions in his own study, noting the decline in voter participation that characterized the 1972 and 1976 presidential elections and the steady decline in party identification that dates from 1940.

Janowitz also discusses the frustration of civil service reform, in which little progress has been made toward improving the administrative effectiveness of the civil service. He sees civil service becoming "an even more effective pressure group" which will "further fragment the control of the governmental agencies by elected officials."

The combination of these political and governmental trends can only increase the "packaging orientation" of contemporary politics with its emphasis on spot television advertisements, perceptions of "leadership," and dwindling opportunities for citizen involvement. Further, these trends will serve to insulate government employees from the policy control of elective officials. As politics increasingly becomes a spectator sport, even at the local level (with declining willingness of citizens to serve on boards and commissions), government may become increasingly reliant on the self-direction of its unionized work force. Within these bureaucracies, a continuing struggle between forces of careerism and planning will unfold—the first aimed largely at the extension of the power and perquisites of civil servants, the second at the decisive intervention of government in the amelioration of complex social and economic problems.

The declared intent of the Republican administration to divest the federal government of its historic (albeit partial and piecemeal) role of fostering societal change and development is surely misleading rhetoric. Change is a continuous product of government, whether it is change aimed at the achievement of new visions or change directed to recapture past images. On any issue over which people disagree, a decision not to act is itself an action. Questions of empowerment appear to be most central among these issues of "direction of change" for the United States in the 1980s.

Empowerment

A consistent theme in U.S. political and social history has been the extension of individual and group rights. One by one, barriers to the full participation of minorities and other victims of discrimination have been assaulted and finally reduced, if not eliminated. Thus, in this century, women have won both the vote and the right to claim economic advancement, though not yet an equal claim on economic resources; the poor have gained access to a still uneven floor of income and service to protect them from inflation's ravages; and the elderly have won increases in Social Security and medical care, though not a full measure of financial security or personal respect from their juniors.

The extension of these rights usually is accompanied with a price tag, in the form of added well-paying jobs, services, or programs to transfer income. The cost of all welfare programs increased from 10.5 percent of the GNP in 1965 to 20.4 percent in 1976. This cost has generally been borne by society at the cost of a portion of the increasing real income of established elites. Because disposable income has increased, the cost has been politically acceptable, though increasingly unpalatable, to those whose taxes have been applied to such social programs. In 1961, 40 percent of the population favored increased welfare spending; in 1975, less than 25 percent expressed such support. Between 1976 and 1979, the proportion of the GNP spent on welfare programs declined to 18.5 percent.

The 1980s, we have seen, may well not be a decade in which real income will advance. The absence of the accustomed "social dividend" may well lead to a retrenchment of the U.S. welfare state, rather than its continuing advance. Economic writer Leonard Silk notes that "if those with stronger bargaining power and scarce skills claim larger shares of a slowly growing national income, and weaker groups, such as blacks and Hispanics, are held back, social and political conflicts will be aggravated." The decision by the Reagan administration to remove a substantial portion of support from society's weaker groups and individuals appears to have greatly raised the probability that these conflicts will be profound in the years ahead.

POLITICAL FUTURES

The combination of governmental and empowerment themes suggests three possible lines of development.

A Continuity Future

Politics increasingly becomes a media event, as party loyalty and rates of voter participation continue to decline. Within government, two images contest mightily: one that conceives of government as *planner*, responsible for assuring the achievement of national goals in a time of resource depletion and socioeconomic instability; the other that views government as *ally* of established socioeconomic and corporate interest. The fields of the contest will be many (especially energy, arms production, environmental protection, and income redistribution).

Declining living standards occasioned by energy shortfall retard the redistribution of income and power toward groups discriminated against by past and present practice—blacks, Hispanics, women, Native Americans, elders. Each of these groups falls further behind the levels of income, wealth, and power enjoyed by white male-headed families, although each group continues to see a minority of its members achieving great success in the nation's mainstream. Movement organizations (such as National Association for the Advancement of Colored People, La Raza, National Organization for Women, American Indian Movement, Gray Panthers) continue their efforts to advance group interests and are regularly joined by new militant groups focusing on direct action. Continued efforts are made to organize a challenging political party centrally representing those excluded interests, and by the year 2000, the People's party wins forty-six House seats, enough to serve as a swing force on party-line votes.

A Good Luck Future

Participation rates, both for voting and other citizen initiatives, do not decline significantly, and party realignments lead to the presentation of clear policy alternatives to the citizenry. Within government, the "planning" conception clearly predominates over the "ally of interest" view. Government is recognized as an effective collective agent of problem resolution in society.

In a modest expansion of the U.S. welfare state, small gains in real per capita income are shared with the most disadvantaged. Political leadership and a resurgence of voluntary leadership emphasize social concern and the reduction of inequalities of wealth and income as a continuing national priority.

A Hard Luck Future

Government moves increasingly toward its *de facto* control by corporate and organizational elites, and citizen participation is reduced to, at best, the occasional act of voting. Nearly all senators are selected from the ranks of millionaires (up from 29 percent in 1981), legislation overrides citizen participation requirements, and the primary criterion for the evaluation of programs becomes its congeniality to corporate preference.

Declining living standards occasioned by inflation, high unemployment, and energy shortfall give rise to explosive levels of intergroup relations, particularly between whites and nonwhites. Urban and suburban riots, random violence, assassinations, and group violence are recurrent and give rise to restrictive "minority policies" of preventive detention, deportation, and surveillance.

VOLUNTARY ACTION: BAND-AID OR CHANGE-AGENT?

Societal happiness, the great French sociologist Durkheim suggested, is a function of the balance that exists between expectation and achievement. The malaise and turmoil that have characterized recent U.S. history may be reduced by lowering our expectations of how much personal happiness we may receive from major social institutions. Alternatively, our societal institutions may be restructured to provide a greater level of reward for their citizen participants. It is the task of the voluntary sector—self-help, altruism, charity, volunteerism, citizen participation, social movements—to mediate between the demands and needs of citizens, on the one hand, and the capacity of institutions to meet those demands and needs, on the other.

Voluntary action provides a way for citizens to organize themselves to advocate, achieve, and provide for themselves without necessarily waiting for the political or economic system to get around to meeting their needs. Amitai Etzioni has called that society in which such action flourishes the "active society." Such a vision is threatened from numerous sources in contemporary America. In the eyes of many scholars, centralization of power in the hands of a number of large corporations is one such threat to the autonomy of democratic decisions of government. Powerful special-interest groups, some of them citizen-based and aimed at single issues, are also seen by some observers to threaten the ability of the system to achieve decisions that balance many interests. Such forces jeopardize the achievement of the kinds of reasonable compromises required for the functioning of a complex, multidimensional society. Finally, widespread apathy and withdrawal from voting and other forms of social and political participation also raise barriers to the achievement of an active society.

Over the past several decades, massive programs of community action, job training, and urban revitalization have had as their most visible effects the raising of expectations of a "clientized" sector of the population and the provision of employment to many thousands of social service workers, among whom are many from minority groups and ideological backgrounds who were formerly excluded from or not attracted to social service. The infusion of the perspectives of these newcomers into the helping professions has contributed, along with the spread of a general skepticism in society, to an increasing level of dissatisfaction with the quality of service-delivery in almost every profession from mental health to education, from medicine to urban planning.

A climate of skepticism has encouraged the development of efforts to implement principles of self-help in the delivery of services. There is every indication that this tendency will intensify in the years ahead. Whether it involves encouraging assertive responses by patients to medical prognoses, the organization of community free schools and public alternative schools, or the evaluation of services provided by lawyers or teachers, self-help is a form of voluntarism that directly contributes to the individual's economic and physical well-being. Self-help also often provides a social context in which both community and consciousness may develop. It may well be the frontier for the development of an active society in the 1980s.

VOLUNTARISM FUTURES

A Continuity Future

Full achievement of an active society continues to be inhibited by corporate power in governmental decision-making, the power of single-interest groups and their unwillingness to compromise, and the widespread apathy of many citizens. The struggle by political, voluntary, and cultural institutions to achieve parity with the corporation remains a continuing theme in American life over the coming decades.

The outcome of this process is the continuation of substantial corporate control in U.S. politics (through the assumption of power by corporate elites and the continuing influence of corporations on policy, regulation, and contractual undertakings), voluntary action (through control of charitable contributions by the United Way and corporate volunteerism), and cultural life (through the media).

A Good Luck Future

Political, voluntary, and cultural institutions increase their autonomy in relation to corporate structures, thus strengthening the active society. New systems of participatory decision-making and management are developed throughout the society, and a reversal is noted in trends toward nonvoting, privatism, and apathy.

A Hard Luck Future

Increasing corporate control over the U.S. polity, voluntary sector, and cultural institutions ushers in a era of struggle between corporate adherents and those outside this sector: the underemployed, individual and small-business persons, students, and defenders of pluralist democracy. A cycle of perceived revolutionary threat and preventive suppression of dissent ensues.

3

Alternative Energy Futures

Modern society, it has become increasingly apparent, is a "zero-sum" enterprise, in which the gains of one person, group, or interest are achieved at some cost to other individuals, groups, or interests. Institutional factors such as those discussed in Chapter 2 are closely interrelated in such a society. The health of one area of effort is often dependent upon developments in other realms of concern.

This chapter seeks to interrelate the societal elements developed in Chapter 2 by combining them into alternative scenarios of the U.S. future. These scenarios each cast energy patterns in a primary position, and so the chapter concludes with a presentation of alternative energy scenarios and a consideration of their relative plausibilities and probabilities.

THREE SCENARIOS FOR THE AMERICAN FUTURE

Scenarios are integrated and coherent perspectives on future societal development; they are based on a systematic demonstration of the interrelationship between various factors of which they are comprised. The construction of scenarios suggests various forms the future might take under different circumstances. It also suggests the ways in which each critical factor can make its mark in affecting the future by showing patterns of feedback and direction change.

Since it has proved possible, and perhaps plausible, to construct three alternative futures for each of the institutional sectors, the point of departure for creating scenarios is to combine their elements around Good Luck, Continuity, and Hard Luck futures. If, indeed, these elements are linked together along such lines, three scenarios will emerge (see Figs. 3.1, 3.2, 3.3).

Let us begin with the Good Luck future and see how the elements

Figure 3.1

A Good Luck Scenario

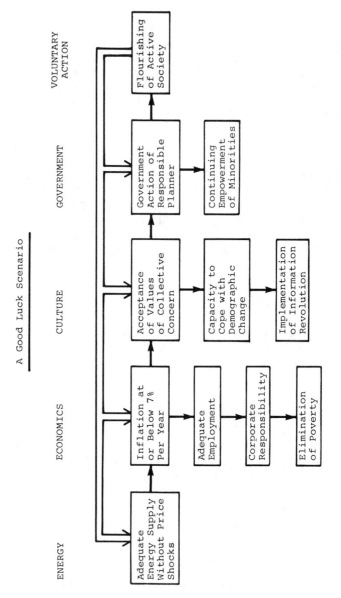

relate to each other. The Good Luck factors, it will be recalled, are:

Energy	Adequate supply without price shocks
Economics	Inflation below 7 percent
	Adequate provision of employment
	Development of corporate responsibility
	Elimination of poverty
Culture	Steady acceptance of values of collective concern
	Capacity to cope with demographic change
	Implementation of information revolution
Government	Development as responsible planner
	Extension of minority empowerment
Voluntary Action	Flourishing of active society

When these elements are arrayed, it becomes apparent that they are closely linked and can be formed into a coherent and integrated scenario. Favorable energy developments can be linked to moderate inflation, which in turn may restore values of collective concern. These factors, in turn, may encourage the development of government as responsible planner, the capacity to deal with demographic change, adequate employment, corporate responsibility, minority empowerment, and the elimination of poverty. The net effect of all these favorable developments will be the achievement of an active society, which will itself reinforce this stable and productive scenario.

Figure 3.1 depicts the linkages. Not only does each of the variables directly contribute to the others as one moves from left to right across the scenario, but also significant feedback loops occur. Institutional strength further enhances values of collective concern, which themselves contribute to the control of inflation. Even the element of energy supply may be brought under at least partial control by adequate institutional functioning and economic predictability; energy conservation and the development of renewable resources may be enhanced by a climate of interpersonal trust and institutional stability.

The Hard Luck factors may be arranged in a similar pattern, with equally plausible results. It will be recalled that the factors identified for each of the elements as Hard Luck outcomes are:

Energy	Severe shortfall and dislocation in pricing

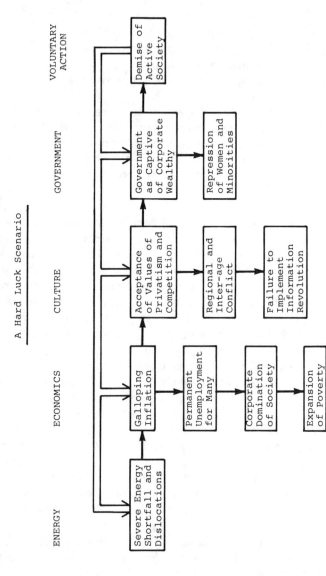

Figure 3.2

A Hard Luck Scenario

Economics	Inflation above 30 percent
	Increasing long-term unemployment
	Corporate domination of economy and government
	Increasing poverty and inequality
Culture	Triumph of values of privatism and competitiveness
	Increasing regional, interage and intergroup conflict
	Failure to implement information revolution
Government	Captured by the corporate rich
	Attempted repression of revolutionary challenges
Voluntary Action	Demise of the active society

Figure 3.2 demonstrates the linkages between these factors in a Hard Luck scenario. This scenario is identical in the placing of the factors to the Good Luck scenario. However, in this scenario each factor contributes to the worsening of each other factor, as the feedback loops assure an ever-deepening cycle of societal and personal frustration and despair.

Now let us turn to the interrelationships between the elements of the Continuity future. These elements are:

Energy	Occasional shocks in price and disruptions in supply
Economics	Inflation steady at 10 percent
	Worsening of unemployment through 1990, followed by some reduction
	Continuing corporate influence restrained by government
	Little change in distribution of wealth and income
Culture	Continuing struggle between materialism and transformation
	Moderate regional reallocation of population
	Implementation of information revolution
Government	Continuing struggle between image as "planner" or "servant of elites"
	Slowing of minority empowerment

Figure 3.3

A Continuity Scenario

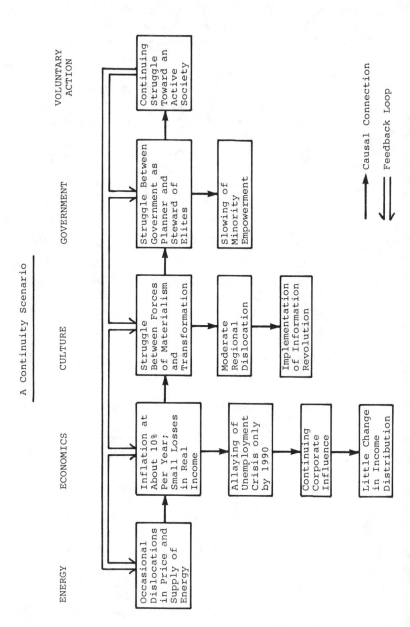

| Voluntary Action | Continuing struggle to achieve "active society" |

Figure 3.3 presents these factors in a Continuity scenario and indicates the lines that may be drawn between societal forces contributing to the strengthening or the weakening of U.S. democracy in the years ahead.

On the one hand, cultural factors of transformation and governmental forces striving toward planning are seen to contribute toward the strengthening of an active society. In opposition to these forces, three other factors (slowing in rates of empowerment, increasing unemployment, and continued corporate domination), together with those forces within government oriented toward the service of elites, are seen to retard the advance of the active society. Since the flourishing of an active society contributes strongly to development of attitudinal forces of meaning rather than those oriented entirely toward material advancement, and since these feelings themselves are seen to affect inflationary outcomes, the importance of this struggle is substantial.

The Continuity scenario differs from the other two in that it posits an indeterminate or continuing struggle at several key points — specifically in the resolution of dominant values, governmental style, and the achievement of an active society. Thus, this model is more open-ended than the other two.

The indeterminacy of the Continuity scenario may represent the U.S. future more adequately then either of the more clear-cut scenarios, the Hard Luck and the Good Luck conceptions. Americans are deeply divided among themselves on a number of fundamental issues: the relation between government and the economy, the direction of income redistribution, the continuing empowerment of minorities, and the method best suited to restrain inflation. It is quite possible that none of these issues will be decisively resolved in the twentieth century.

The depth of the frustration felt by many Americans with our national inability to resolve the above issues was well reflected in 1981 by the support received by President Reagan for a policy of "trying something new." However, the risk was great that the new policy would prove highly inflationary, and thereby its prospects were also great for precipitating a future closely resembling the Hard Luck scenario. It also appears unlikely that progressive forces will be permanently subdued. Social and political forces committed to an active and autonomous government, continuing income redistribution from richer to poorer, continuing minority empowerment, and restraint of inflation by direct government action will remain active. Thus, the prospect is substantial for continuing conflict and lack of resolution on these central social and political issues.

If the Continuity scenario does hold sway, the year 2000 will see a persisting standoff between forces of materialism and other-relatedness and between government as planner or government as steward of elites. The quest for the active society will continue; issues of redistribution will remain problematic. These issues may not clearly be resolved until we are well into the twenty-first century. Yet they surely are questions that will continue to excite the commitment and concern of many citizens and organized political, economic, and social forces.

It will be noted that a primary factor in each scenario involves energy availability—and it seems apparent that the supply of energy and how we use it are destined to determine much of our societal future. If energy is indeed a primary variable in social development, potential dislocations in its supply and form can be anticipated to have profound consequences. It would seem only prudent, then, to delve more deeply into the ways in which our energy future might be directed, for such decisions will have grave consequences for many other aspects of our lives in the years ahead.

Once more, the tool we shall use in charting these alternative futures will be the scenario. Several large-scale and systematic energy scenarios have been developed in recent years and provide perspective on the range of possibilities we may confront in our energy future.

IMAGES OF ENERGY SUPPLY

Working through 1974, the Energy Policy Project of the Ford Foundation developed three scenarios of future energy supply for the United States. More recent research of Denis Hayes, the Workshop on Alternative Energy Strategies, and Amory Lovins suggests that true no-growth or even declining-supply scenarios might usefully be contemplated as possible visions of the future. Such scenarios have been developed in recent years by the Friends of the Earth, the author of this book, and the Committee on Nuclear and Alternative Energy Systems of the National Academy of Sciences.

The Ford scenarios involved:

1. Pre-1973 trends projected. Orderly transition occurs from oil to coal to eventual exploitation of breeder technology. There is continued growth in energy use of 3.5 percent per year.
2. Modest growth (1.9 percent per year) toward a viable multibased future, including nuclear energy. There is orderly transition from oil to coal to nuclear energy—with increased development of renewable sources. A conservation strategy, aimed at reducing waste, permits continued economic expansion with largely unchanged patterns of energy usage.
3. Steady state of energy availability after 1990. Limited growth occurs in the energy supply until 1990, then it levels off, with oil replaced by coal and renewable sources. A conservation strategy is accompanied by increasing demands on energy from industrial and household sources.

To this list, we will here add two more scenarios, one for no growth, and a second showing a decline in energy supply.

4. Steady state of 1977 level of usage through year 2000, and beyond. The development of renewable sources begun in late 1970s continues to permit orderly transition. A conservation strategy is accompanied by dramatic decline in per capita use of energy.
5. Decline to 75 percent of 1977 level of usage by year 2000, with even grimmer future prospects. A failure to develop renewable energy occurs. Frequent crises develop with the exhaustion and failure of multiple energy sources and supplies.

The amount of energy available under each scenario needs then to be distributed among the basic users of energy: transportation, residential, and industrial-commercial. Present trends show a pattern of energy usage that allocates 20 percent of the total to household uses (primarily heating and cooling), 25 percent of the total to transportation, and the remainder to commercial and industrial usage. These proportions are unlikely to prevail in the future because of differences in elasticity that will attach to energy growth and decline. It may be, for example, that transportation usage will prove to be highly elastic in the case of energy decline, whereas household heating and cooling usage will prove to be relatively inelastic. The proportion available for new construction appears moderately elastic (in theory) and certainly is subject to variations in public policy. Dantzig and Saaty, for example, foresee a total energy savings of 15 percent in their *Compact City,* almost all of which is garnered from reductions in automobile usage.

On the other hand, it is clear that the amount of energy savings that could potentially be achieved in residential heating and cooling is considerable. Krenz has recently demonstrated that savings between 40 and 50 percent can be achieved through the redesign of almost every energy-driven device, and Phillips and Stobaugh and Yergin have shown that savings of 40 percent can be achieved in energy use by most householders. A combination of weatherizing, moderation of temperature, and introduction of flue-dampers is capable of reducing home energy use well below its present 20 percent of all energy use. One may still question the will of the homeowner and renter to achieve these savings, however. The 40 percent (or more) reduction remains a theoretical possibility and goal, rather than an actual achievement.

If Americans must make a forced choice of loss of energy for transportation, heating, and industrial-commercial use, transportation may prove to be the one most greatly curtailed in the event of energy shortfall. In such a situation, savings in home heating and cooling may approach the 40 percent goal only following a time-lag of many years, as homeowners and renters only gradually achieve the many small but arduous tasks required for those savings. An even lesser shortfall in business and industrial energy use begins to cut deeply into the availability of jobs, as the experience in the cold winter of 1977 demonstrated. Thus, by elimination, of the three uses, transportation is most likely to be cut immediately and cut deeply.

But what of new construction in a time of shortfall? Will not this be the right time for the development of energy-saving housing on a large scale? For better or worse, insufficient energy would be available in a time of shortfall for the sort of crash building program of more-energy-efficient new cities envisaged by Soleri, Small, and Dantzig and Saaty. Such schemes, Percival Goodman asserts, should be consigned "to the Museum of Architectural Curiosities. . . . How interesting it will be for future historians to see renderings and models of those mile-high, miles-long megastructures in which dwelling places are plugged in, clipped on, or otherwise arranged for ready removal to suit the latest fashion." The bottom line is, Goodman asserts, that "the world cannot afford such schemes."

What can we afford as our habitat in an energy-short future? By necessity, it would appear to be largely the one we have already built for ourselves, modified and rationalized wherever possible within the limits of affordability. In such a future, policy makers will seek to maximize the usage of existing shells and will approve new construction only on a modest basis, placing a higher priority on energy conservation than on extensive reconstruction. In the event of energy shortfall, we shall have to rely primarily on the stock of shells we have in existence for our basic residential, commercial, and industrial needs.

Table 3.1 presents the likely amount of energy available for transportation, residential use, and industrial-commercial use under each of the five energy scenarios. What is most striking about the Ford scenarios (the first three) is the variability of industrial-commercial energy use under differing growth conditions. Fully 61 percent of the energy increment between the first two scenarios, 59 percent between the second and third, and 103 percent between the third and 1973 levels are predicted to be allocated to industrial and commercial use. This pattern differs dramatically from that of the other two uses: Energy for residential use is seen to grow only marginally from 1973 levels under the second and third scenarios, and energy for transportation is seen to decline from present levels in the third scenario. The Ford planners clearly hold the belief that our energy priorities lie in industrial and commercial growth, and their logic is accepted in the construction of the fourth and fifth scenarios.

Under conditions of steady-state energy use, and of energy decline, the two shortfall scenarios envision a determined attempt being made to protect overall economic health at the direct cost of a radical decline in energy available for transportation. This assumption is consistent with that of the Ford planners and leads to the conclusion that the level of energy for transportation would fall 36 percent below present levels in the fourth scenario and 52 percent below present levels in the fifth scenario.

The implication of a possible 52 percent decline in energy for transport is that an even greater decline will ensue in energy available for automobile consumption. Table 3.2 presents the Ford predictions showing that energy for transportation must be shared among seven major categories of use, each of which has different elasticities.

Of the seven major transportation competitors for energy, the Ford planners see three as highly elastic: automobiles, buses, and airplanes. Truck use is seen as moderately elastic, and energy use for rail, farm machinery, and ships is viewed as highly inelastic. Transportation energy, after all, is used both for passenger transit and the shipping of freight, and the latter purpose is more inelastic in the

Table 3.1

Energy Available in Year 2000 for Major Purposes, Under Five Scenarios

	Pre-1973 projected	Modest growth	Energy use Steady state after 1990	ZEG† from 1973	Decline to 75% 1973 levels	Comparison-1973 pattern
Transportation	38.4	24.7	17.2	13.5	9.0	18.8
Residential use	30.1	19.3	17.0	15.0	14.0	16.3
Industrial-commercial	118.2	80.0	65.8	46.5	33.25	39.9
Total	186.7	124.0	100.0	75.0	56.25	75.0

(in quadrillion BTU's)

†Zero energy growth

Source: Jon Van Til, "Spatial Form and Structure in a Possible Future," _Journal of the American Planning Association_ (July 1979). By permission of the publisher.

Table 3.2
Transportation Energy for Scenarios (Year 2000)

	Scenarios			
	Pre-1973 projected	Modest growth	Steady state after 1990	Actual 1975 levels
Auto	15.2	6.8	3.8	10.0
Bus	0.2	0.2	1.0	.02
Air	11.6	8.2	4.1	1.9
Truck	6.5	4.4	3.7	4.2
Rail	1.7	1.9	1.7	0.7
Farm machinery	1.5	1.5	1.5	1.1
Others (ships)	1.7	1.7	1.4	1.0

(In quadrillion BTU's).

Sources: Jon Van Til, "Spatial Form and Structure in a Possible Future," Journal of the American Planning Association (July 1979). By permission of the publisher. The Ford study predictions are found in the Ford Foundation, A Time to Choose: America's Energy Future (Cambridge, Mass.: Ballinger, 1974),p.475.

event of energy shortfall. Fitting these assumptions to the fourth and fifth scenarios produces the data presented in Table 3.3.

The energy trade-offs required for the last two scenarios would be among the most difficult political decisions made in U.S. history and would surely require a rationing system for users. Table 3.4 shows how one way of reorganizing transit might affect individual mobility.

In scenario 5 (75% decline) presented in Table 3.4, an attempt has been made to maximize the miles traveled per person by greatly expanding individual bus and train use while reducing the use of the more energy-wasteful forms of transportation—personal automobile and airplane travel. Such an expansion in bus and train use would require twenty-four-hour-a-day service, full utilization of capacity, staggering of work hours, and a crash program of bus construction. Even with these changes, however, the total travel achieved would decline by over 25 percent from 1970 levels. Were the automobile relied upon more heavily, the travel loss would be even more substantial.

Table 3.3
Transportation Energy for Scenarios 1–5 (Year 2000)

	(1) Pre-1973 projected	(2) Modest growth	(3) Steady state after 1990	(4) 1973 ZEG	(5) 75% decline	Actual 1975 levels
Auto	15.2	6.8	3.8	2.0	1.0	10.0
Bus	0.2	0.2	1.0	2.0	1.75	0.2
Air	11.6 (6.2)	8.2 (4.3)	4.1 (3.0)	1.9**	.5**	1.9 (1.34)
Truck	6.5	4.4	3.7	3.5	2.0	4.2
Rail	1.7 (.09)	1.9 (.11)	1.7 (.16)	2.0 (.3)	2.0 (.3)	0.7 (.04)
Farm machinery	1.5	1.5	1.5	1.1	1.0	1.1
Others (ships)	1.7	1.7	1.4	1.0	.75	.10
Subtotals						
Energy for transit	21.69	11.41	7.96	6.2	3.55	11.58
Energy for freight	16.71	13.29	9.24	7.3	5.45	7.52

Energy available for passenger transport is italicized; other energy is for transport of freight (in quadrillion BTU's)
** No air freight.

Source: Jon Van Til, "Spatial Form and Structure in a Possible Future, "Journal of the American Planning Association (July 1979). By permission of the publisher.

SHRINKING IMAGES OF POSSIBILITY

Viewed from the perspective of the early 1980s, the two shortfall scenarios just described seem better than what may realistically confront us in the years ahead. As David R. Brower has demonstrated, the limits of the thinkable in energy planning have permitted the plausible postulation of increasingly constrained visions of the future. The Sierra Club's estimate of U.S. energy needs of 140 quadrillion British thermal units (BTU) by the year 2000, presented in 1972, was viewed as heresy. But by 1978, committees of the National Academy of Sciences were working with heretical estimates of 67 to 77 Quads. Amory Lovins's forecast of 125 Quads was seen as simply beyond the pale when presented in 1972. By 1978, the Friends of the Earth were presenting 33-Quad scenarios.

Although it has become increasingly possible to "think small" about energy futures (or "think big" about energy shortfall), few scenarios for the year 2000 that envision more than a 25 percent decline in energy availability have been developed.

One scenario that conceives a future in which energy availability might fall to barely more than 33 percent of present levels has been published by Friends of the Earth. This projection involves a reduction of energy use to 46 percent of 1975 levels by the year 2050. Savings are projected in four energy uses—residential, commercial, transportation, and industrial—and the largest cut is predicted for personal transportation, where per capita use is seen to involve a 77 percent savings. The Friends of the Earth rely upon a doubling of miles per energy unit and a reduction in vehicle use to achieve this goal.

Energy-short scenarios have not only emerged from the environmentalist and conservationist camps but also have been constructed by the scientific and political establishment in its embodiment in the National Academy of Sciences.

Reporting in 1980, the academy's Committee on Nuclear and Alternative Energy Systems presented six scenarios, of which the most pessimistic envisioned a drop in supply to 58 Quads by the year 2010. A comparison of these scenarios with those just presented shows great similarities, especially in the total supply predicted and the use projected for transportation. However, a comparison between our two shortfall scenarios and the committee's images of shortfall shows a distinct difference in the energy forecast for the heating and cooling of buildings.

Whereas our most energy-short scenario foresees that 14 of 56.25

Table 3.4
Travel in Miles Per Capita for Five Scenarios (Year 2000)

	(1) Pre-1973 projected	(2) Modest growth	Scenarios (3) Steady-state after 1990	(4) 1973 ZEG	(5) 75% decline	Actual 1970 levels
Auto	9410	9410	7570	3784	1992	8210
Bus	255	255	1365	3938	3448	240
Air	4190	3905	1955	1238	326	780
Rail	125	410	590	1106	1106	60
Totals	13980	13980	11480	10066	6872	9290

Major assumptions:
1. *For scenario 1*
   a. In autos, 1.4 persons per vehicle in cities; 2.4 in rural travel.
   b. For autos, urban fuel economy of 10.4 miles per gallon.
   c. For buses, 15 persons per vehicle-mile.

2. *For scenario 2*
   a. For autos, fuel economy of 25.0 miles per gallon.
   b. For planes, increase passenger load factor by from 54% to 67%.
   c. For planes, reduce flight speed to permit 4.5% reduction in fuel use.
   d. For rail, tripling of passenger-miles per available seat.
   e. Assumptions 1a, 1c above.
3. *For scenario 3*
   a. For autos, fuel economy of 33 miles per gallon.
   b. Six percent of population in new towns, requiring 50% auto usage.
   c. Ten percent of urban traffic carried by bikeways and walkways.
   d. For buses, 19.5 person-miles per vehicle-mile.
   e. Replace plane trips of 400 miles or less by train travel.
   f. Assumptions 1a, 2b, 2c, 2d above.
4. *For scenario 4*
   a. For buses, 30 person-miles per vehicle-mile.
   b. Assumptions 1a, 2b, 2c, 2d, 3a, 3b, 3e above.
5. *For scenario 5*
   a. Assumptions 1a, 2b, 2c, 2d, 3a, 3b, 3c, 4a above.

Source: Jon Van Til, "Spatial Form and Structure in a Possible Future," Journal of the American Planning Association (July 1979). By permission of the publisher.

Quads might be devoted to residential use by the year 2000, the academy foresees the allocation of 6.4 Quads of a total of 58 for the similar needs of the "building sector" by the year 2010. This remarkable savings of 62 percent from 1975 levels may seem as radical as our 15 percent might appear conservative.

The academy's Demand and Conservation Panel explains its forecast, which is conditional upon a fourfold rise in energy prices and a full commitment to energy conservation:

> New energy-efficient appliances find ready markets, and solar energy begins to make a significant contribution near the end of the period (2010): 25 percent of new air conditioners, 50 percent of new space heaters, and 70 percent of new water heaters in 2010. Improved retrofit measures and construction practices contribute to the energy savings use in this scenario. . . . [The shortfall scenario] assumes continued migration to sunbelt states and acceleration of trends to multifamily units. These changes reduce heating and cooling requirements by about a third. Additional savings are achieved by the use of integrated utility systems in residential complexes to cogenerate electricity and heat.

A second massive study of the year 2000 emerged in 1980 in the Global 2000 Report, prepared for President Carter by the Council on Environmental Quality and the Department of State. Reviewing a number of energy studies, the Global 2000 Report finds that for the entire world

> the supply situation will tighten rapidly over the 1980–90 period, with a strong possibility of real price increases caused principally by OPEC resource conservation policies that limit production. In the long range, a further tightening in the oil supply situation can be expected due to resource depletion effects. This resource problem is characterized by two phenomena:
> 1. The world appears to be facing a long-run oil and gas depletion situation, because reserve additions to the production base may not be sufficient to support the growth in demand.
> 2. The growth rates of energy consumption will have to fall substantially from currently projected levels to be consistent with projected rates of growth in resource production.

Applying these trends to the United States, the report concludes:

> • U.S. oil and gas production from conventional resources will

be unlikely to cover the growth in U.S. oil and gas consumption.

- However, the rate of growth of U.S. consumption can be cut dramatically in the long run by aggressive conservation policies.
- At least to the year 2000, the contribution of technology—supply enhancement, synthetics production, nuclear generation, and renewable resources—will not make up the excess of U.S. energy demand over supply, and U.S. dependence on world oil resources will continue at least at the current range of 7–10 million barrels per day.

PERSISTING IMAGES OF PLENTY

Even images of energy plenty have begun to be cast in more conservative terms. When the Exxon Corporation presented its 1980 forecast, for example, it projected an annual growth rate in energy use of 1.1 percent per year through the year 2000. The previous year's projection by the same corporation anticipated a yearly increment of 3.5 percent.

A more systematic large-scale study of energy futures, published in 1979, was prepared by a team at Resources for the Future, a Washington, D.C., research institute. This report takes a fundamentally optimistic view of our energy future, seeing it as a problem in societal management rather than resource exhaustion. Like David Stockman, it trusts in the ability of the free market to assure our energy future.

> The higher price of energy is neither a crisis nor the essence of the energy problem. If we can manage the adjustment to a new era of energy scarcity, the higher prices may be the solution to the energy problem. A sensible energy-pricing policy can help us manage the many adjustments that must be made by providing the incentives to make the substitutions that are possible. With these higher energy prices, future energy demand levels may be much lower than might be expected from the historical trend.

Thus, the Resources for the Future group finds it "incorrect and misleading to define the long-run energy problem in terms of a gap, shortfall, or shortage, as though there were some natural definition of energy needs and some physical supply limits preventing these needs from being met. The energy is there to be had, at a cost, in virtually whatever quantities it may be demanded, and demand itself is a variable," as the quote above argues.

The fundamental optimism of this perspective is revealed in the report's prediction that "in the long run of half a century or more, some of the more speculative forms of energy production, such as nuclear fusion and new applications of solar energy, will in all likelihood be capable of supplying *essentially unlimited* amounts of energy at *costs* that will probably be high, but easily manageable with the income levels of that time" (emphasis added).

Clearly, the Resources for the Future group is betting heavily on good luck in our energy future, on continuities in energy availability, and on societal wealth. It recognizes that we might bungle our way into less desirable futures through mismanagement of our wealth, but it fundamentally denies that scarcity will be the problem.

Further support of the position held by Resources for the Future may be drawn from an extensive review of energy policy by the Pulitzer Prize–winning team of investigative reporters, Donald L. Bartlett and James B. Steele. The United States does not have a coherent energy policy, Bartlett and Steele argue, but "has instead energy anarchy—a jumble of conflicting, contradictory, and often counter-productive laws, regulations and programs that pass as policy."

Taken as a whole, the reporters argue:

> This morass of laws and rules working at cross-purpose has assured that:
> - Americans will face still higher prices for all forms of energy—from gasoline to electricity.
> - The nation will remain indefinitely vulnerable to supply disruptions by hostile foreign oil producers.
> - Most of America's abundant energy resources will remain frozen deep in the ground and concentrated in a few hands—hands that are in no hurry to develop them.

Central to the analysis of Bartlett and Steele is that the United States is energy-rich. Like Office of Management and Budget (OMB) Director Stockman, they note that proven reserves cited by oil companies have steadily kept pace with production over the past decades. They suggest that oil companies have done their best to keep estimates of reserves as low as possible, thereby encouraging the most rapid price rises possible. Projecting government and industry data, they arrive at the astounding estimate that the United States has enough crude oil, natural gas, shale oil, geopressured methane, and coal to feed our current energy appetite for 847 years! Such sources will steadily be "discovered," they imply, when the energy companies find it in their interest to "announce" these "finds."

ONCE MORE, PASCAL'S WAGER

The point should now be obvious: For projections of energy futures one pays one's money and takes one's choices. The various visions summarized in this chapter range from drastic shortfall to astounding bounty.

On April 12, 1981, *The New York Times* described the results of a two-year study conducted by the Rand Corporation for the U.S. Geological Survey and the Department of Defense:

> A two-year study for the Federal Government has concluded that the prospects of finding more oil and gas in the United States are severely limited. Future discoveries will be considerably smaller than most analysts have predicted, the study says, and output will fall faster than expected.
>
> . . . the report says that as of the end of 1979, 121 billion barrels of oil had been discovered in the United States, and it said there was a 50 percent probability that 20 billion more barrels would be produced as a result of new discoveries. In contrast, six other reports cited by the Rand researchers contain estimates on new oil discoveries ranging from 55 billion to 161 billion barrels.

The summary of the Rand study goes on to note that our chances of drawing more than 36 billion barrels of oil from existing reservoirs are also below 50 percent, as are our chances of finding more than 170 trillion feet of natural gas (570 trillion cubic feet have already been discovered). These predictions lead to estimates of twenty to forty years remaining for domestic oil production and seventeen to twenty-six years for natural gas.

The Rand researchers report that the limits we face with oil and gas are geological, not economic. Most oil is found in large pools, and most of these pools have been found.

On the same day on which the Rand study was reported, *The New York Times Sunday Magazine* also contained a pessimistic assessment of the prospect for nuclear power's expansion, written by Anthony J. Parisi, an energy reporter serving as an editor of the *Petroleum Intelligence Weekly*. Economics explains the weakness of the nuclear future, Parisi asserts, not technology. He describes a "vicious spiral" at work:

The utilities insist their customers will need more electricity than their customers turn out to want. The outsized projections make nuclear power appear unavoidable. But to build all those costly new plants, the companies exhaust their borrowing power and seek large rate increases. The big increases further slow the growth in demand for electricity, so the companies once again start hacking away at their construction programs. And the first proposed plants they cut are the most troublesome and most expensive to build — the nuclear-powered ones.

By the time the reader's eye meets this page in print, reports of further projections of our nation's energy future will doubtless have been completed and released, and of such reports, there will be no end. Some will surely be optimistic, and others will be gloomy in their outlook. Whatever new data or perspective these reports may bring, the possibility will remain that the supply of oil, gas, nuclear energy, and coal will not sustain our current life style and that the shortfall will subject us to a series of jolts and shocks. Our Pascal's wager on energy remains before us.

4

The Variability of Urban Form

The spatial destinies of cities are set by millions of individual decisions made over long periods of time. The spatial patterns to which these decisions give rise have an endurance of their own. To be sure, it is often possible to blot out the structures of the past, as Los Angeles did when it removed its interurban streetcar lines. But, even then, a vestige of the original pattern remains in that freeways now course along many of the original streetcar ways.

Among the principal factors that determine the spatial patterns of our cities and towns is energy—its availability, its forms, and its prices. To understand how the face of the United States might be changed in an era of energy shortfall and transformation, it is first necessary to understand how it came to its present appearance.

SPATIAL FORM AND STRUCTURE

This chapter begins with the contemporary landscape of the United States and the ways people have built upon it. Looking at the form and shape of a city, town, or suburb, the viewer quickly becomes aware that these settlements spread across the continent possess distinctive shapes of their own. These varying shapes are apparent to residents and urbanists alike. Kevin Lynch has shown in his studies of how people perceive cities that key elements of their form, such as central landmarks and boundaries between neighborhoods, are stored in the mental maps that most residents carry with them of the places in which they live. Urban sociologists and geographers, initially convinced that a single pattern of urban form could be determined, have more recently come to conclude that metropolitan forms are multiple and vary with local forces and choices in the city's development process.

The classic work on the form of U.S. cities and suburbs was done by sociologist Ernest Burgess, who described in a chapter in the influential text, *The City,* a circular zone theory of urban spatial form.

> The typical processes of the expansion of the city can best be illustrated, perhaps by a series of concentric circles, which may be numbered to designate both the successive zones of urban extension and the types of areas differentiated in the process of expansion.
>
> This chart represents an ideal construction of the tendencies of any town or city to expand radially from its central business district – on the map "The Loop" (I). Encircling the downtown area there is normally an area of transition, which is being invaded by business and light manufacture (II). A third area (III) is inhabited by the workers in industries who have escaped from the area of deterioration (II) but who desire to live within easy access of their work. Beyond this zone is the "residential area" (IV) of high-class apartment buildings or of exclusive "restricted" districts of single family dwellings. Still farther, out beyond the city limits, is the commuters' zone – suburban areas, or satellite cities – within a thirty- to sixty-minute ride of the central business district.

When other urbanists sought to apply the Burgess zonal model to their own cities, different patterns of urban form sometimes provided a closer fit. Maurice Davie found, for instance, that New Haven was more accurately understood by using a radial model, or what Homer Hoyt would later call a "sector" model. In this image of urban form, major land uses clung to arteries of transportation as they led to and from the city's core, forming a wedgelike pattern of land use. Support also emerged for what Harris and Ullman called the multiple nucleus theory, in which major functions of land use were seen to develop throughout the metropolis.

Many U.S. cities had grown in ways reflecting a combination of the sector and radial theories, as Hoyt's study of the shifts in fashionable residential areas demonstrated. As Figure 4.1 shows, the middle class had moved to the suburban ring with the development of the streetcar and the automobile and had tended to follow the radial lines out from their initial settlements.

Gradually, urbanists came to the conclusion that the circular zone theory was particularly well suited to the understanding of Chicago's form, but was hardly a universal model of the modern metropolis. Many cities, it became clear with time, were required to make room for heavy industry within their boundaries. Chicago was unique in seeing its industrial work force employed in nearby Gary, In-

FIGURE 4.1

Shifts in Location of Fashionable

Residential Areas

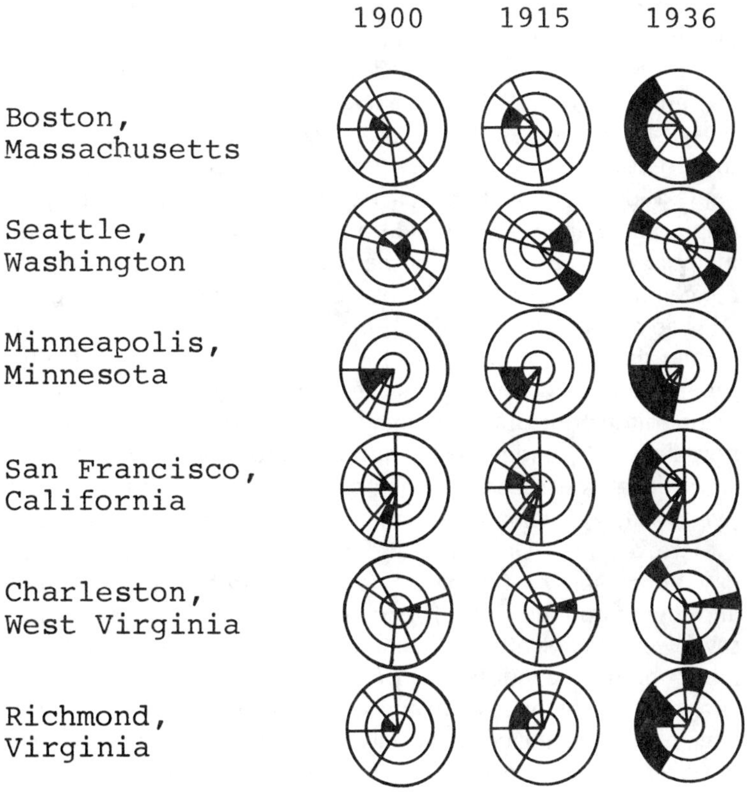

	1900	1915	1936
Boston, Massachusetts			
Seattle, Washington			
Minneapolis, Minnesota			
San Francisco, California			
Charleston, West Virginia			
Richmond, Virginia			

Source: Homer Hoyt, The Structure and Growth of Residential Neighborhoods in American Cities (Washington, D.C.: Federal Housing Association, 1939), p.115.

diana—beyond the map of the pioneering Burgess and his students.

A highly useful way of viewing the shape of the contemporary metropolitan area was developed by Catherine Bauer Wurster in 1963. Recognizing that the structure of these areas varied greatly, Wurster depicted them as varying along two separate dimensions: first, concentration to dispersion, and second, region-wide specialization to subregional integration. Fitting spatial patterns in the United States to the dimensions, Wurster derived four possible future paths for the development of the city: (1) present trends projected, (2) general dispersion, (3) concentrated supercity, and (4) constellation of relatively diversified and integrated cities (see Figure 4.2).

The four types she developed identify four predominant options that are well grounded in empirical reality and/or planning theories. The first type, present trends projected, shows a marked tendency toward dispersion, with a lesser degree of concentration, all within a context of region-wide specialization. The second type, general dispersion, is the vision of metropolitan sprawl that characterizes so many newer Sunbelt cities of the United States. The third type, the concentrated supercity, is the one envisaged by visionary architects like Paolo Soleri and Glen Small, in which a population density much greater than that of present-day Manhattan is accommodated in an urban megastructure. Finally, the fourth type, constellation of relatively diversified and integrated cities, involves more concentration than the present form, but also provides a high degree of subregional integration, allowing particularly for a close location between spatial systems of residence and employment.

More recently, David Gordon has distinguished between three developmental forms of the U.S. city: the commercial, the industrial, and the corporate city. The commercial city developed in the seventeeth and eighteenth centuries to meet the needs of a mercantile economy; the industrial city developed in the nineteenth century as a reflection of the need to concentrate workers' residences around large plants; and the corporate city has emerged in two basic forms in the twentieth century to meet the needs of a series of interrelated bureaucracies.

When platted on the pre-existent capital base of an old industrial city, the corporate city's downtown has taken the characteristic form of a collection of corporate skyscrapers, surrounded by empty manufacturing areas and former working-class residential areas that have become ghettos. Modern industries are located in the suburbs, along with the homes of middle-income persons; the rich live even farther away from the old metropolitan core.

Figure 4.2
Four Alternative Paths of Development for the City

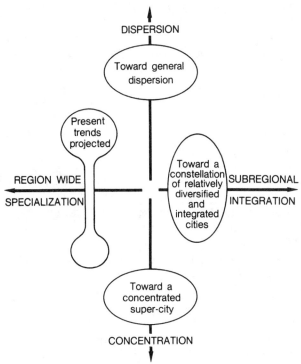

Source: Catherine Bauer Wurster, "The Form and
Structure of the Future Urban Complex," in
Lowdon Wingo, Jr., ed., Cities and Space
(Baltimore: Johns Hopkins University Press for
Resources for the Future, Inc., 1963), p.48.
By permission of the publisher.

In its Southern, Southwestern, and Western forms, the corporate city has been able to develop unencumbered by extensive
nineteenth-century building. Constructed largely from scratch, it is
the fragmented metropolis: without a clear downtown, without
working-class housing districts, but with economic activity every-
where.

Gordon's scheme parallels Wurster's typology at three points: the
corporate city on an industrial base (that is, the Northeastern city)
with type 1; the corporate city on its own base (that is, the Sunbelt

city) with type 2; and the commercial city with type 4. Gordon argues that urban form is not an inevitable outcome, but is rather a variable, subject to the control of human planning and institutional choice.

In presenting his theory of the economic determination of urban form, Gordon suggests that twentieth-century urban development has followed the preferences of corporate leaders to disperse working-class residents (thereby reducing the threat of organized dissent), to reduce local taxation on corporations, and yet to retain necessary transportation and communication links to markets and other structures (by travel, car, and telecommunications). His theory implies that the needs of corporate structures will continue to affect the form of settlement patterns.

To get a fuller image of Gordon's three models of the U.S. city, the reader may imagine himself or herself on an airplane approaching Philadelphia or Los Angeles. The latter destination brings the twentieth-century corporate city par excellence into view; the former shows traces of several centuries' impact.

As Los Angeles is approached over buildable land (from the southwest), the traveler begins to see an alternating pattern of land use between open-range land and tract-home development. The principal feature, however, is the omnipresent freeway paralleling the plane's path to the metropolitan core. Soon the freeway intersects a second freeway, and a distant glance shows that these "ribbons of white" form a great web that knits the various segments of the metropolis. On the northern side, they penetrate a substantial range of mountains; to the west, they trace paths just inside the ocean's shore; to the east, they cross high mountains toward the distant desert.

The traveler begins to note that the intersection of each pair of freeways often is surrounded by intensive land development—shopping centers with expanses of parking space, industrial centers, office buildings of five or more stories, and apartment complexes. Beyond these centers of development extend the finer strands of surface arteries and suburban streets. Within that web can be discerned many of the one and one-half million single-family homes in which the majority of the residents abide. In some neighborhoods, behind almost every one of these "dots," the traveler discerns a spot of blue that is the private swimming pool.

As the plane proceeds toward the geographical center of the conurbation, one searches in vain for the pattern of intensified land use that characterizes so many cities that were platted before the twentieth century. But here the pattern is more gradual, and the dominant feature remains the linked freeways and the neatly ordered rows of homes. To be sure, the clumping of larger buildings becomes more pronounced, and these centers do not always surround the freeway interchanges. But the search for a single core of great buildings and intensive land use reveals numerous contestants for the core. None is clearly predominant.

The approach to Philadelphia also takes the traveler over great multilaned highways, but their paths are askew from the route toward the urban core. One highway passes to the north, another the east. Indeed, only two freeways penetrate the metropolis to any degree, forming an elegant script "Y" through the area. Nowhere is the interwoven latticework of the Los Angeles freeways visible.

The transition to urbanism in Philadelphia is gradual. The green of rolling hills and farmland, dotted with small towns, yields slowly to the presence of country estates. The towns become larger and more frequent, and an occasional shopping mall comes into view. Soon, suburban development begins to dominate the view, but little consistency is apparent from point to point in yard size or house type. The keen observer, however, will see the larger homes scattered about invisible radii from the metropolitan core—which radii, the ground observer will note, turn out to be railroad tracks for commuter trains.

As the flight continues toward Philadelphia's core, great industrial plants are seen along the shore of the two great rivers of the area, which themselves parallel the two major freeways in the script "Y" below. On landing, the traveler may learn that the freeways were not only built to parallel the rivers' courses but also were named for them.

Before long, the suburban pattern yields to a grid of streets lined with row houses, a pattern broken only by an occasional park, commercial street, or industrial sector. As the plane begins to traverse the urban core in a great circle, the buildings rise in height in a pattern that resembles the movement from foothill to peak in a circular mountain range. At the center stands City Hall, whose height may be exceeded, informal convention decrees, by no other building in the city. In each direction radiate other buildings just a few feet shorter. At the edges of the core, a series of grid streets surrounded by small houses once more appears.

To summarize the observations made during our simulated flights, Los Angeles follows the corporate model and Philadelphia combines commercial, industrial, and corporate forms.

Los Angeles was desert in the heyday of the commercial city and shows nothing of that model. It was founded in the age of the industrial city, as a series of small towns in a great valley—linked by a system of interurban trolleys. Save for the fact that some freeways were constructed over the courses of those now-defunct trolley lines, little remains of that nineteenth-century structure save place names and certain points of cultural interest.

Los Angeles stands today the creature of the automobile and the twentieth-century corporate city. It is the city of the multiple nuclei, sewn together by the ingenious threads of its freeways, contained in its boundaries only by the mountains and the sea. Only in recent years have attempts been made to build a dominant urban core, but this center will continue to be one of many such nodes of activity in this decentralized metropolis.

Philadelphia, on the other hand, shows clear remaining traces of the impact of each of the three models and remains fundamentally shaped as it was in its earlier decades. As one of the great commercial walking cities of the early eighteenth century, its legacy of townhouses between the rivers, dotted by the regular placement of green squares, remains today in the jewel neighborhoods of Philadelphia's "revitalization": Society Hill, Washington Square West, Fairmount, and Center City.

Equally apparent is the nineteenth-century industrial model in neighborhoods that still today show the two-story workingman's row houses clustered on narrow streets around the city's factories, which ring the core in most directions and are especially evident along the rivers' edges. Indeed, in the Germantown area, which blossomed following the introduction of the horse-drawn streetcar in the 1850s, the homes of workingmen, middle managers, and factory owners are still readily apparent. So are the upper-middle-class residential suburbs that surround the commuter stations of the suburban railway lines. Both are creatures of the nineteenth century, although many of the new suburbs were founded a century before as independent towns beyond the city's reach.

The twentieth century also makes its mark on Philadelphia. Corporations have built there to meet their communication and production needs. In the suburban areas, corporate centers surround the few intersections of limited access highways, at King of Prussia and Exton, for example. Within the metropolis, substantial development has also occurred outside the reach of the city tax assessor; several substantial suburban nodes have developed, on City Line Avenue and in New Jersey's Cherry Hill, for example. But much corporate activity takes place at the metropolitan core, and new buildings are regularly added to the forest surrounding Billy Penn's hat on the top of City Hall. The center holds even though the economic imperatives alter.

The difference between the forms of Philadelphia and Los Angeles cannot be described in terms of population density only, although more Los Angelenos live in single-family homes than do Philadelphians and Los Angeles has a somewhat lower population density than Philadelphia. Nonetheless, for years Philadelphia and Los Angeles have ranked high among large U.S. cities in the proportion of their population that resides in single-family homes, and the population density of Los Angeles is greater than that of the average U.S. city today. The major differences between these metropolises involves their urban forms per se: Philadelphia remains concentric while Los Angeles is multinucleated.

Between the two forms of development represented by the Sunbelt cities of the West (from Denver to Phoenix to Los Angeles) to the Eastern cities (from Boston to Charleston) lie the hybrid cities of the South and Midwest—formed in the nineteenth century and adapted for the twentieth. These cities grew as transportation links between the industrial East and the expanding frontier. Today, they more nearly resemble the spread pattern of the West than the centralized one of the East. They are crossed by at least one freeway and often circled by its bypass. Their urban cores are largely unpopulated, and suburban centers of industry, business, and commerce proliferate around them. Their inner neighborhoods are homes to the poor; the wealthy still prefer the suburban regions. Nonetheless, centers of apartment and condominium construction show a modest trend toward middle-class residence in certain centrally located nuclei in these cities.

The direction of spatial development in the U.S. experience has been steadily toward population deconcentration and spread. The question of its future direction regards the continuation of this process. Will the city of the twenty-first century be even more dispersed than the corporate city of the twentieth century? Or will future patterns of spatial development see some tightening of the boundaries of cities and towns? These questions will be addressed with continuing reference to the work of Wurster and Gordon in the remainder of this chapter and the next.

Of particular interest in this inquiry is the scale of our future settlements. Will we live in great metropolitan complexes in which our places of work, interaction, and recreation are widely scattered? Or will we find ourselves in communities in which our lines of transportation will be more substantially reduced? It has been a powerful or-

thodoxy in urban studies that scale will increase and that metropolitan development will continue to aggregate on the edges of urban areas. This orthodoxy bears careful reconsideration in a time of
resource constraint.

THE THEORY OF INCREASING SCALE

The forces that shape our cities and towns are often viewed as
beyond the control of any human institution. When Ernest Burgess
developed his concentric zone theory of the city at the University of
Chicago, he was strongly influenced by the thinking of his mentors
and colleagues in what came to be called the "Chicago school of urban studies." Particularly influential in defining this perspective were
Robert Park and Louis Wirth.

Park viewed the city from the point of view of "urban ecology,"
which as he developed it was an extended analogy between the city
and a living organism. Cities, in this perspective, formed the turf on
which the competitions among the human species were performed.
Ethnic groups, racial groups, holders of differing values and life styles,
and social classes all struggled to assert their control of space—to find
their "niche" in the urban order. Powerful forces of ecological succession were seen to control the use of space, such as invasion, conflict,
competition, and assimilation.

To the urban ecologist, the city was a congeries of "natural areas,"
in which the needs of groups were fitted to the opportunities provided by the city. These opportunities can be viewed by the contemporary eye as basically economic in their orientation. Indeed, the approach of the urban ecologist is one of economic determinism of
space, though an economic determinism closer to the Darwinian acceptance than the Marxian call for change.

What is most important to the present argument is the dual assertion of the Chicago school that, first, city form is crucial to the
achievement of individual and group goals and, second, it is fundamentally beyond the reach of purposive human action to control
or reshape. These principles of importance of form and its uncontrollability were underscored by Park's assertion that life was lived at
two levels—the cultural and the biotic. Institutions of culture could
be created and revised by human beings; biotic structures were a
part of our natural order. Cities, of course, were placed in the biotic
category.

The grip of spatial determinism has been somewhat loosened in the
urban studies of the past half-century, but the core recognition of the

Chicago school that urban form is heavily influenced by socio-economic forces not easily controlled by citizen or policy preference remains widely accepted. So does the assertion that the spatial shape of our society is important to individual and group interests.

Contemporary urbanists no longer distinguish between cultural and biotic forces, and they refer to "social," rather than "natural," areas. Nonetheless, they tend to retain the belief that powerful forces of urbanization and modernization are abroad in our society, forces that retain the irreversibility and uncontrollability with which the Chicago sociologists cloaked the forces of urban ecology.

The conventional wisdom of contemporary urbanism ascribes to the concept of "increasing societal scale" a potency akin to the Chicagoans' ecological determinism. Perhaps the most firmly established finding of today's urban studies is that increasing societal scale accompanies urbanization and modernization; another widely accepted belief is that scale will continue to increase throughout the remainder of the twentieth century and on into the foreseeable future.

Societal scale is customarily defined in terms of space and physical mobility. Thus, Friedmann and Miller have defined the "urban field" as "a fusion of metropolitan spaces and nonmetropolitan peripheral spaces centered upon core areas (SMSA's) of at least 300,000 people and extending outwards from these core areas for a distance equivalent to two hours' driving over modern throughway systems (approximately 100 miles with present technology)." Friedmann and Miller note that their definition of urban fields includes between 85 and 90 percent of the total U.S. population and assert that "as the area of metropolitan influence is substantially enlarged, nearly all of us will soon be living within one or another of the 70-odd urban fields of the United States."

The theory of increasing societal scale takes Wurster's schema of urban forms and turns it into a theory of societal development. As societies modernize, the theory asserts, dispersion and specialization increase. Thus, the city of the future comes more and more to resemble Los Angeles, replacing its commercial and industrial structures and neighborhoods with the tracts and freeways of the spread metropolis. The more Marxist of these thinkers will accept Gordon's statement of fit between increasing scale and corporate need; the more bourgeois thinkers will explain the increase in scale in terms of societal preference. In either case, the assertion is made that increasing urban and social scale appears to be an ongoing and irreversible process.

If the theory of increasing scale determines our urban future, the options for spatial adjustment to a limited energy future will be constrained. It is therefore important to understand why our spatial patterns have emerged as they have, in order to see what sorts of choices we may realistically anticipate being faced with in the years ahead.

Discussions of urban development over the past few centuries have focused on the role transportation has played in the expansion of urban scale. This history has been reviewed in the earlier discussion in this chapter. But what of contemporary patterns of spatial change? Do they show the inexorable extension of scale? Or do they, rather, suggest that spatial patterns are shaped by an interaction between resources and preferences?

If the future of urban scale is to be established as a variable factor, subject to control and reversal, two assertions must be demonstrated. First, it will have to be shown that present trends do not document the unfolding of irreversible forces, but rather evince the consequences of human choice. Second, it must be demonstrated that a reversal of tendencies toward increasing scale is at least theoretically possible in the future. The remainder of this chapter will focus on present trends; the following chapters will consider the future.

PRESENT TRENDS IN URBAN SCALE

A review of current trends in the spatial patterning of U.S. cities, suburbs, and towns may be summarized in five propositions.

First, the decentralization of population continues as suburban population continues to grow at a more rapid rate than urban population.

Second, the "counterurbanization" of population appears to be accelerating as an increasing number of metropolitan areas (cities and suburbs) show absolute declines in population size.

Third, decentralization continues to characterize all major economic activities, with the exception of manufacturing, which appears to be neither recentralizing nor decentralizing.

Fourth, many central cities remain in fiscal distress, and people in them are in severe socioeconomic straits; there is little indication that these problems will be greatly ameliorated by what "revitalization" of cities is currently underway.

Finally, interruptions in energy supply, increases in energy prices, and concern with energy futures have not made a perceptible impact on the form of the U.S. landscape.

These propositions and the evidence supporting them are presented in the ensuing pages. The chapter will conclude with a consideration of the possibility that these trends may be modified in the years ahead.

Suburbanization

The tendency of population to increase less rapidly in central cities than in their suburban rings has been firmly established in U.S. metropolitan areas since the 1920s. From the 1920s to the 1960s, growth in the suburban rings of our Standard Metropolitan Statistical Areas (SMSAs) has proceeded at a pace exceeding growth in the central cities of these areas. Indeed, by the 1960s, the population in the suburban rings came to exceed the population contained within the central cities.

In the 1970s, for the first time in our history, central city population is actually in decline, while the pace of suburban growth continues its upward climb, though at a slower pace than it achieved in previous decades. Figure 4.3 shows the pattern of urban and suburban population change throughout the twentieth century. Certainly within metropolitan areas, population continues its move away from central neighborhoods.

Counterurbanization

The actual decline in central city population, both in real terms and as a proportion of national population, underwrites the power of suburbanization in contemporary U.S. development. Indeed, the combination of these population losses with the slowing of suburban growth has given rise to an unprecedented pattern of metropolitan development, which has been called *counterurbanization*.

For the first time in U.S. history, census data released in the late 1970s indicates that metropolitan population is in actual decline in one major area of the country, the Northeast, and has leveled off to a nearly changeless state in another, the North Central area. Only in the South and West is metropolitan growth continuing, and only in the South is metropolitan growth proceeding at a more rapid rate than the growth of population in nonmetropolitan areas (rural areas and small towns). Nationally, the rate of population growth within metropolitan areas increased 5.5 percent between 1970 and 1977; the corresponding rate of growth in nonmetropolitan areas was 9 percent during the same period.

Brian Berry, who has coined the term *counterurbanization*, sees it as the result of processes of declining birth rates, increasing migration

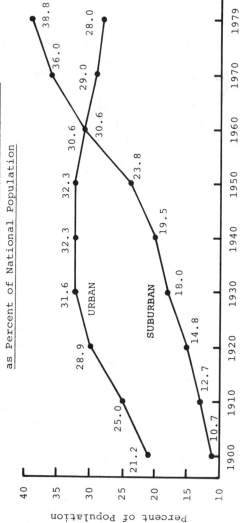

Figure 4.3

Urban and Suburban Population in the 20th Century,
as Percent of National Population

Sources: For 1900 to 1950, Alvin Boskoff, The Sociology of Urban
Regions (New York: Meredith, 1962), p. 52; for 1960, Joseph S.
Vandiver, "Urbanization and Urbanism in the United States," in Faud
Baali and Joseph S. Vandiver, eds., Urban Sociology (New York:
Meredith, 1970), p. 50; for 1970, John Kramer, ed., North American
Suburbs: Politics, Diversity, and Change (Berkeley: Glendessary
Press, 1972), p. xiii; and for 1979, The New York Times (November 2,
1980).

flows to the South and West, and the migration flow toward nonmetropolitan areas. He notes that we now experience "(a) absolute population declines in the majority of the nation's largest central cities; (b) a slowing of the growth and onset of decline in some of the other metropolitan regions of the northeastern snowbelt; (c) continued growth of smaller and intermediate-sized sunbelt metropolitan regions; and (d) the onset of new growth in the nonmetropolitan regions throughout the nation." Of this new nonmetropolitan growth, Berry estimates that one-third results from "overspill" from metropolitan development and two-thirds from new development outside of accustomed metropolitan growth areas.

Counterurbanization has given rise to population losses in such diverse metropolitan areas as New York, Los Angeles–Long Beach, Philadelphia, Detroit, Washington, D.C., Cleveland, St. Louis, Pittsburgh, Cincinnati, Buffalo, Newark, Jersey City, Dayton, and Akron between 1970 and 1977. Though these cities may be in the process of becoming the "mature metropolis" described by Leven, they are clearly not being chosen by Americans as their favored places of residence.

Don Dillman has summarized the findings of a large number of recent studies of residential preference and concludes that a "population turnaround" is in process.

> The available evidence clearly shows that Americans prefer, other things equal, to live in more rural locations than where they presently live. The imposition of severe income and commuting constraints diminishes, but by no means eliminates, interest in rural living. Other research indicates rural preferences have been increasing during the past decade and that some Americans have been able to follow their preferences. . . . But the strongest evidence that residential preferences are contributing to the turnaround is not the results of any one study; instead it is the striking consistency among the results from all studies.

Counterurbanization is in full swing and is apparently fueled by the conscious preferences of many Americans. Once more, the process of increasing scale is apparent.

Economic Decentralization

As the population of the United States has steadily drifted into suburban and nonmetropolitan locations, so has its economic base decentralized. One-third of the manufacturing jobs within SMSAs were located in the suburban ring in 1948; by 1972, more than half these jobs were suburban. Wholesale employment grew even more rapidly in the suburbs, its share rising from 8 percent in 1948 to 43 percent in 1972. And so it was with services (from 15 percent to 37 percent) and retail jobs (from 25 percent to 53 percent) over the same period.

Some researchers have found evidence to indicate that the flight of manufacturing to the suburbs has ended. Solomon notes that the proportion of manufacturing jobs located in the suburbs declined from 51.8 percent to 51.1 percent between 1963 and 1972, and Haren and Holling claim that although rural and other nonmetropolitan areas added 1.8 million manufacturing jobs, or 56 percent of the national increase between 1962 and 1978, more than half that gain occurred by 1967 and practically all of it before 1974. However, Black suggests that "the loss of manufacturing from central cities has accelerated and has even infected most suburban rings." Between 1970 and 1975, ten areas he studied showed "a net loss of 312,000 manufacturing jobs from their central cities and a net loss of 67,000 jobs from their suburban rings. . . . On average, the cities lost one of every five manufacturing jobs existing in 1970 while the suburbs lost one of thirty." Black's ten SMSAs are all large in population, however, and include only one Western (Denver) and one Southern (Atlanta) city.

To make sense of these different claims one must set these data in the context of the different regions of the country. While all studies indicate that employment in the Northeast grew far more slowly over the past two decades than in the South and West, with North Central employment in between, McKenzie's data show a striking recovery in the Northeast since 1972. He not only finds no difference in total employment growth among the regions between 1972 and 1978, but he also finds that manufacturing employment has increased far more rapidly in the Northeast during that period than in any other region. Whether that recent growth has been concentrated to a greater extent in metropolitan or nonmetropolitan regions is difficult to determine, but it is clear that the flow of employment to the Sunbelt was largely stalled in the 1970s. It is also clear that Sunbelt gains have never resulted from substantial immigration of firms from the Northeastern and North Central states, but rather reflect a higher birth rate of firms in the South and West and a higher death rate among larger firms in the Northern industrial tier, a factor noted in the policy conclusions of the Northeast-Midwest Congressional Caucus.

It may be too early to count the Northeastern and North Central states out of the business of providing employment, particularly in manufacturing. It is also too soon to count out the metropolitan areas in relation to their nonmetropolitan competitors. Employment gains remain more rapid in the metropolitan areas than in the nonmetropolitan areas in the South. In the West and North Central states employment gains during the past decades have been substantial but slightly less in the metropolitan areas than in the nonmetropolitan areas. The employment slump in the Northeast was reversed in the 1970s, with a substantial metropolitan recovery demonstrated in the 1977–1978 period of economic growth, in which the traditional employment centers recorded a growth of 100,000 manufacturing jobs. While there are no clear signs of a resurgence of urban employment's domination of the manufacturing arena, there are signs that patterns may be leveling off. The theory of increasing scale is less clearly supported by the evidence regarding economic location.

Fiscal Distress

The tendency of some societal observers and analysts to employ the term *urban* as a code word for such terms as *poor, black, minority,* and *economically depressed* does not advance our understanding of cities or urban life. As clear-headed observers of urban life now quite sharply contend, cities vary greatly in the degree to which they are centers of distress or delight. Most are a combination of both.

Recent work by Harvey A. Garn and Larry Clinton Ledebur of the Urban Institute is most helpful in clarifying the variability of urban distress. Examining data from the nation's 147 largest cities, they find that the national growth rate in per capita income was not achieved in almost three-fourths of these cities. Moreover, analysis of urban economic performance, defined as a function of change in the number of jobs, unemployment rates, and per capita income levels and their rates of change, indicates that high interrelationships exist between poor economic performance and two other variables: city size and regional location.

Regionally, distress is concentrated in New England (where all cities analyzed are among the most distressed), the Middle Atlantic region (where 94 percent of the cities analyzed rank among the most distressed), and in the East North Central region (where 44 percent of the cities are so ranked). In no other area of the country are more than 12 percent of the cities rated among the most distressed. Thus, Garn and Ledebur clearly establish the regional specificity of urban distress from data generally drawn up to 1975: Urban distress exists in the Northeastern region and in Ohio, Indiana, Illinois, and Michigan; it is not prevalent in the rest of the country.

City size is also dramatically related to economic distress. The 6 cities over 1 million in population are most severely distressed; the 49 cities between 250 thousand and 1 million are less severely distressed; and the 92 cities between 100 and 250 thousand are in the most advantaged financial condition.

Garn and Ledebur also examine the fiscal distress of urban governments and develop an index that includes such factors as long-term debt, common-function expenditures, tax burden, and changes in the last two variables. They find that the "economic and fiscal performance indicators are positively correlated, but the correlation is not high." They therefore caution that public policies directed at the alleviation of cities' fiscal distress may not be the best response to their economic problems, and the opposite may be inferred as well.

Garn and Ledebur identify a number of cities that rank in the lowest quintiles on both economic and fiscal distress. With three exceptions (Buffalo, Cincinnati, and Atlanta), the list reads like the Amtrak timetable from Washington north: Baltimore, Philadelphia, Newark, Jersey City, Paterson, New York, Yonkers, New Haven, Hartford, Springfield, Worcester, New Bedford, and Boston.

Three factors are sometimes cited to suggest that the fiscal decline of the Northeastern city may be checked: the return of manufacturing, the gentrification of certain urban neighborhoods, and the coming pinch in energy pricing and supply. The first factor has been considered above, and the evidence there cited suggests the possibility of some post-1975 recovery. The third factor is a major theme of this book. Gentrification, the second factor, will be considered next.

Perhaps Franklin James of the Department of Housing and Urban Development has pushed available evidence to the most committed position:

> A number of journalists and commentators have mistakenly concluded that the recent upsurge in reinvestment in older central-city housing may solve many of the pressing social, economic and fiscal problems of declining cities. In large part, this hope is unjustified and misleading. . . . Available evidence, though scanty and sometimes anecdotal, suggests that the new demand for older housing is almost nonexistent in some metropolitan areas and widespread in others.

James notes that urban reinvestment has not been experienced in such declining cities as Pittsburgh or St. Louis, where housing demand is itself depressed. He concludes that "without effective public encouragement, many of the severely distressed cities of the North and the Midwest are unlikely to be much affected by the new, more intense demand for older homes and the revitalization it can bring."

Other students of urban revitalization are less willing than James to conclude that the city will not benefit financially from gentrification. Laska and Spain identify an emergent issue of the 1980s: "Will revitalization become a large enough trend to alter the economic plight of cities, or will we see a growing tension between the dual processes of disinvestment and reinvestment?"

On balance, then, the economic picture is not bright for a number of larger Eastern cities, especially those in which neighborhood revitalization is not present and manufacturing remains in decline. However, these cities form only a minority of the nation's cities, and the possibility certainly remains that a combination of governmental programs and economic breaks might lead to their eventual stability.

As with economic decentralization, the theory of increasing scale draws support in the area of fiscal distress, but that support must be qualified to some extent.

Energy Impacts

The final factor related to the theory of scale concerns the impact on spatial patterns of the energy dislocations of the 1970s: the disruptions in oil supplies occasioned by international turbulence in 1974 and 1979, the shortages of natural gas in the fearful winter of 1978, and a steady escalation in the rise of energy prices. The automobile industry was brought to its knees by shifting consumer preference for gasoline-efficient cars. New interest was shown in energy conservation and the development of alternative energy sources to the fossil fuels that had served so centrally in the twentieth century.

Despite these substantial effects on the U.S. economy brought by changing energy patterns, urbanists have discerned few changes in spatial patterning that result from these changes. Thus, at the peak of the gasoline shortages of 1979, *The New York Times* interviewed a number of leading urbanists who tended to agree with Herman Kahn that "energy has gone from cheap to inexpensive" and that "on the average life style will remain unchanged." Said Bernard Frieden of Massachusetts Institute of Technology (MIT), "There is very little evidence that the middle class would move back to the cities. . . . I expect to see overweight colleagues riding bicycles before they give up their suburban homes."

Papers presented to the President's Commission for a National Agenda in 1980 by leading urbanists repeated the same themes. John Kasarda of the University of North Carolina set the pattern by referring to "an emerging footloose economy" that continued to open jobs in "deconcentrated suburban and exurban settings."

The most detailed studies of spatial consequences of energy dislocation in the 1970s were conducted by Dale L. Keyes. In a series of simulation studies, he demonstrated that household energy savings in a typical urban home, with its shared wall space, amounted to about 30 percent over the energy expenditures in the typical suburban home. Savings between 25 percent and 50 percent were anticipated for the average homeowner moving from a suburban to an urban location. Keyes concluded that these savings, while obviously substantial, will be less attractive to individuals than the alternatives of reducing the amount of fuel used for transportation and achieving greater efficiency in automobile usage. Moving from suburban to an urban location "is likely to incur the highest transaction costs and be the most disruptive to a family's way of life."

Thus, for the 1970s and the immediate future, the weight of evidence indicates that energy dislocations are not affecting spatial patterns and choices. The theory of scale is apparently not yet deflected by changing energy patterns.

IS INCREASING SCALE IRREVERSIBLE?

The review of five elements of the theory of increasing scale lends, overall, support to the contention that the theory remains a strong explanatory and descriptive force for contemporary urban dynamics. But what of the future? Is increasing scale actually irreversible? Or is it rather a pattern of development nearing its reversal?

Dale Keyes argues that increasing scale is likely to continue: "Gains in personal income are likely to blunt the edge of increases in the price of energy. Only if the price of fossil fuels rises severalfold in real terms is it likely that major structural changes to urban areas will appear. And a price change of this magnitude is most improbable, even in light of the most pessimistic assessments of existing fossil fuel resources." Keyes declines the Pascal's wager, but leaves open the slim possibility that things might work out differently. But he is not joined by all prominent urbanists in that judgment. Speaking bluntly of the possibility of an energy-short future, David Burch of MIT has said: "I am very suspicious of any obvious answers. Realistically nobody knows anything." What we must decide, however, is the wisdom of thinking seriously about, and preparing for, the actual possibility of an energy-short future, however slim that possibility may be.

To assess the likelihood that urban scale will continue to increase, it is important to ask two questions: First, is increasing scale fueled by factors beyond human choice and control? Second, are any of the trends that contribute to increasing scale irreversible?

The five trends we have just examined — suburbanization, counterurbanization, economic decentralization, fiscal distress, and lack of energy effect — certainly do not lie beyond the realm of human decision and choice. If Gordon and Dillman are both correct, the form of the twentieth-century metropolis and its surrounding areas have been chosen by concurrence between top societal elites and individual consumers. To consider these choices as belonging in the realm of inevitability is to restore the now-discredited distinction Park sought to make between the cultural and the biotic. People choose the spatial patterns in which we live, though not necessarily in a fashion in which each person's preference registers equally.

As for the irreversibility of the trends, two seem presently in the process of substantial slowing, at least in part. The tendency of manufacturing, a central component of economic structure, to leave urban settings for suburban and nonmetropolitan locations, seems largely to have ceased in the late 1970s. And the return of many middle-class persons to some central cities gives evidence that the fiscal distress of some Northeastern cities may be subject to some improvement. The fact that most cities nationally are not in any serious fiscal distress further indicates that the demise of the city may be prematurely recorded.

From the perspective theory in spatial development, it seems more sensible to view scale as a variable factor, influenced by the preference of urban residents, the needs of important societal institutions, and the resource base necessary to sustain transport, commerce, and amenity within the society.

Once we begin to view scale as a variable, the choice among the hypothetical urban futures outlined by Wurster and Gordon becomes a real one. Will it be

- The corporate city sited on an industrial base, the model of the Northeastern city projected into a future of continuing decline and dispersion?

- The corporate city on its own base, the model of the Sunbelt city projected into a future of continuing deconcentration?
- The concentrated supercity, built to meet the energy and social needs of a gregarious twenty-first-century society?
- The return to the structure of the commercial city, well-integrated regionally and somewhat reconcentrated?
- A yet-to-be-created form that combines centralization and decentralization in ways yet to be discerned, perhaps varying with regional history and climatic factors?

Such a choice will be made by societal actors—institutions and individuals—in concert, although it may not be made in a foresightful or purposive fashion. The choice will certainly be influenced by future energy supplies and configurations, however, and the following chapter turns to a consideration of the impacts these forces may have on our spatial future.

5

Energy: Shaper of Space

The amount of energy available to us and the ways in which we use that supply importantly affect our use of land. Three major propositions have been argued in earlier chapters: First, that the spatial form and structure of the built environment are heavily shaped by energy sources. Thus, the horse-drawn streetcar turned the form of the city inside-out. Metropolitan boundaries have been dramatically extended by the automobile, a creature dependent on cheap oil. Second, that historical trends toward increasing per capita energy availability are slowing; we may well be entering a period of long-term, if not permanent, energy decline. Thus, plausible scenarios of energy shortfall are being constructed by futurists of many energy persuasions. Third, that conservation will be increasingly employed in the use of energy, such that savings of up to 40 percent can be achieved in energy use without significantly detracting from quality of life; in the already built environment, such savings will more commonly be realized in amounts between 15 and 25 percent of current levels. Thus, although our contemporary energy patterns are built on a "cushion of excess," full elimination of this waste will not be achieved in a short period of time. Gasoline-inefficient cars will remain in use for more than a decade until they are retired, and the existing housing stock will turn over at a considerably slower pace.

What is the likely form of spatial settlement in the American future? One major factor must be assessed before predictions can be ventured. This factor pertains to energy itself and particularly its own form and structure, for energy sources, like cities and towns, take different shapes that perform different work. This chapter considers the structure of the various forms of energy that fuel our mobility, heat and cool our homes, and undergird our industrial order. The differences in energy forms and structure have far-reaching consequences for the futures of our cities and towns, including the urban options identified in the previous chapter.

ENERGY FORM AND STRUCTURE

When energy futures are considered, it is conventional to think in aggregate terms. Thus, we add together the various sources of sup-ply—oil, gas, nuclear power, solar energy, and so on—and convert them into equivalencies of barrels of oil or BTUs. This process leads to one final number, the total amount of energy from all sources that will be available in a given year.

Although it is often useful to think in terms of total energy supply, we should also consider the individual types of energy sources; we may thus derive some insight into how we may best use the energy available to us in the future.

There are four major differences between the types of available energy. (1) Some forms of energy can be permanently depleted and some can be renewed. (2) Some forms of energy can be readily used to fuel vehicles and some are less suited to this purpose. (3) Some energy sources produce more pollutants than others. (4) Some sources require central generation or refinement and some may be produced locally.

The first dimension (renewability) distinguishes between fossil fuels (oil and coal) and nuclear fission—nonrenewable energy forms—and hydroelectric, solar, and (theoretically) nuclear fusion—renewable energy forms. Oil and coal take many millions of years to form, and the process cannot be hurried. Similarly, nuclear fission in its present light-water forms converts uranium fuel into energy and waste without renewing the resources being depleted. The various forms of renewable energy, on the other hand, are replenished by the daily cycles of sunlight's fall on the earth. Hydroelectric power harnesses the flow of streams that are renewed by cycles of evaporation and rainfall. Direct and passive reception of the heat of the sun provides many present and potential uses for the heating of homes, buildings, and water; solar energy also has many potential industrial applica-tions. Methane may be collected from the decomposition of plant and animal matter, known as biomass. Alcohol may be refined from corn and sugar plants for use as a liquid fuel. Wind power may be harnessed by mills. Temperature gradients within the seas may be utilized as an energy source. Geothermal heat may be captured as it leaves its underground chambers. The energy of the sun may be con-verted into electricity by small but powerful photovoltaic cells. These and other renewable forms of energy draw on the energy generated daily by natural forces of earthly and solar interaction. Should the controversial nuclear source of fusion energy become developed, it would share the characteristic of renewability with the many solar sources.

The second dimension, ability to fuel vehicles, distinguishes between oil and almost all other forms of energy. Gasoline, the concentrated liquid refined from oil, is well suited to fuel buses, automobiles, and airplanes; however, other sources of energy can be used to power such vehicles. Automobiles can be converted so that they can be fueled by grain alcohol. Electricity can be stored in batteries to power automobiles, and it can also be used to provide power to rails and wires for the movement of trains, trolleys, and some buses. Nevertheless, an enormous commitment in technology and life style has been vested in the gasoline-powered automobile in the modern world. It would be a substantial adjustment in cost and technology to shift our dependence to alternative fuels to move our automobiles.

The third dimension, pollution, is of particular consequence in dense population settlements where it may give rise to discomfort and disease. Here, hydroelectric and almost all forms of solar energy rank low – generating little if any pollution. The pollutants produced by oil, coal, and nuclear fission are widely recognized. They take the form of various oxides, particulates, and radioactive waste and provide substantial problems in the use of these energy forms. It is likely that nuclear fusion, should it ever be developed, would similarly generate pollution in the form of radioactive emissions and the creation of high temperatures of water used in its processes.

The fourth dimension deals with the degree of centralization required for the generation of the major forms of energy. Oil must be refined at large processing centers, and coal, nuclear fission, and other sources used in the generation of electricity are typically consumed in large power stations. Only solar energy, in most of its forms, does not require central generation. To be sure, centralized processes of solar collection are being developed, but this form of energy is well suited to widespread decentralization.

When these dimensions are considered in relation to principal energy sources available (see Table 5.1), four different patterns of energy form and structure emerge: (1) Energy sources that are nonrenewable, nonoptimally suited to fuel transportation, highly polluting or possibly unsafe, and centrally generated. This category includes coal, natural gas, and nuclear fission, in its present forms,

Table 5.1

Characteristics of Major Energy Forms

MAJOR ENERGY FORMS	DIMENSIONS OF DIFFERENTIATION			
	I. Degree of Renewability	II. Ability to Fuel Transportation	III. Pollution	IV. Typical Pattern of Power Generation
Oil	None	High	High (oxides)	General Refinement
Coal	None	Low	High (oxides, particulates)	Central
Nuclear Fission	None to Possibly High (breeder reactor)	Low	High (thermal, safety, radio-active waste)	Central
Nuclear Fusion	Possibly High	Low	Low	Central
Hydroelectric	High	Low	Low	Central
Solar	High	Low	Low	Decentral

Source: Adapted from the author's "Forms and Structure of Spatial Patterns and Distribution," in Energy Resources and Conservation Related to Built Environment (Pergamon Press, 1980), pp. 145-160. Reprinted with permission from Pergamon Press.

applied to the generation of electrical power. (2) Energy sources that are nonrenewable, well-suited to fuel transportation, highly polluting, and centrally refined. This category includes oil and its derivative, gasoline. (3) Energy sources that are renewable, nonoptimal for transportation, possibly unsafe (breeder reactors) and centrally generated. This category includes the two nuclear forms yet to be commercially developed – breeder and fusion sources. (4) Energy sources that are renewable, generally poorly suited for the powering of transportation (but not entirely so), low-polluting, and potentially decentrally generated. This category includes the various forms of solar energy, including hydroelectric, wind power, and direct reception of solar heat – the soft energy paths.

The recent history of energy supply in Europe applies as well to North America:

During the twentieth century and especially in the post-1945 period, there has been a strong tendency in the ECE (Economic Commission for Europe) region to centralize the conversion and distribution of energy resources. In the nineteenth century such centralization was almost totally absent; fuel, in solid form, was delivered to individual homes and other buildings and its conversion – burning – took place at the point of end-use. The change to a more centralized system of supply began with the creation of municipal gas systems in the late nineteenth century, and was enormously increased by the growth in the use of electricity since the beginning of the twentieth century. This extension of the electricity distribution network has been a major task of governments and electricity utilities, a task that was essentially completed by mid-century. Virtually the entire population of the ECE region is now linked to an electricity generation distribution system that is highly centralized and that is becoming continental rather than national in scope in both Europe and North America. . . . Because of the problems of storage, gas is also a fuel that requires an expansive basic infrastructure so that it can be supplied to the point of end-use as required. By contrast, the use of oil is much more decentralized. Like coal, it can be stored safely and conveniently in relatively small amounts close to the point of end-use (e.g., an individual dwelling). Like coal, such storage points can be supplied by a flexible distribution system – oil pipelines, rail and road tankers, etc. – that can be gradually enlarged and extended without, normally, massive investments in fixed infrastructure. The relative simplicity of oil distribution systems, which of course also affects the supply of energy for urban transportation, is a major reason why oil has tended to replace the less convenient coal as the ubiquitous fuel in the ECE region. Just as there are few households without elec-

tricity in the ECE region at present, there are similarly few that do not
have easy access to supplies of oil.

The story of energy in the Western World is one of increasing centralization, pollution, and fueling of vehicles. Renewability is a concern of only the past decade, and it has become a highly controversial criterion.

RENEWABLE ENERGY AND SHORTFALL

The case for choosing to use renewable energy sources wherever
possible has been made by a number of persuasive authors, among
the most prominent of whom are Amory Lovins, Barry Commoner,
and Lawrence Solomon. These authors assert that we should define
the choice between renewable and nonrenewable energy sources as
"forced." Further, they contend that the renewable option is the most
productive one, leading to peace and social justice as well as to
energy adequacy.

Lovins, Commoner, and Solomon point to two major problems in
placing our fundamental reliance for energy supplies upon the hard-
energy path. The first problem is that of resource exhaustion, and the
second is that of vulnerability to disruption of supply. In the short- and
middle-run perspective of the next fifty years, the second problem is
likely to predominate. In the long term of the next several hundred
years, the problem of resource exhaustion will likely prove most
significant.

W. Jackson Davis vividly describes the way in which resource exhaustion intensifies over time and eventually leads to a social crisis of
monumental proportions: "Suppose we are confronted with the task
of finding a finite number of Easter eggs hidden in a meadow of finite
proportion. The likelihood of finding an egg in a given period of time
depends principally upon three variables: the number of eggs, how
well the eggs are hidden, and how hard we look." Davis shows that a
bell-shaped curve will characterize the recovery rate if search effectiveness increases while the total supply becomes increasingly
depleted.

The same logic applies to the discovery of fossil fuels. Eventually,
no matter how sophisticated our technology, the remaining oil will
be too scarce and too well hidden to warrant recovery. Davis explains: "Long before the last barrel of oil is extracted from the earth it
will become uneconomic to remove that barrel. It will take more
energy to extract the oil than is contained within the oil itself." Once

we pass the peak period of energy development, society's institutions will diminish, Davis foresees, unless, of course, renewable sources begin to lay some new energy "eggs."

Oil is only the first of many natural resources whose exhaustion looms on the immediate horizon. Amory Lovins has declared that we are likely to face a water shortage within ten years that may surpass the seriousness of our energy crisis; Richard Barnet and Jeremy Rifkin have described in convincing detail the magnitude of impending shortfalls of many other resources.

Just when the "eggs" of fossil fuel become so scarce that their price exceeds the ability of almost all consumers to afford them cannot be certainly pinpointed, for it depends upon pattern of energy use and the rate at which alternative sources of energy are developed. But the fact that the day of exhaustion will come, at least for oil, seems difficult to deny. Unless fusion power is rapidly harnessed or the soft path is promptly developed, we run the risk of energy shortfall.

By continuing to import many millions of barrels of oil per day, we may choose to retain our policy of hard-path reliance on it, even though it becomes increasingly scarce and costly. A possible (some would say likely) consequence of this choice would involve recurrent interruptions in this precarious supply flow. Some of these interruptions may be temporary in duration, occasioned by the disfavor of a mercurial potentate or the policy swings accompanying a political revolution. Others may be of longer term, accompanying an oil war, blockade, or shift in power-bloc orientation.

One should not assume that war and embargo are the only possible causes of hard-path disruption. Roberto Vacca has detailed, with chilling plausibility, the crisis that could be created by the crash of an airliner into a regional power station during a period of frigid winter weather. Such an accident might precipitate *The Coming Dark Age,* as Vacca titles his grim fantasy, an age in which "the problems of an advanced civilization will be replaced by those proper to a primitive civilization, and it is probable that the majority of survivors may be made up of people particularly adapted to passing quickly from a sophisticated to a primitive type of existence." If civilization is to be preserved in such a future, Vacca asserts, it will be by its nurturance in well-endowed "monastic communities," possessed of such concrete things as "tools, implements, motor-generator sets; nonperishable goods which a monastic community would make more of; goods exchangeable for food, particularly salt, sugar, and alcohol; drills, electric cells, copper wire, stainless steel screws, and small-arms ammunition." Such endowed survival groups, Vacca foresees, "will be found competing ruthlessly with other survivors of every sort gathered in chance clusters."

The societal consequences of an unanticipated and sudden reduction of energy availability are unpleasant to contemplate. The guiding values of American society, as Robin Williams has so persuasively argued, have centered around individualism, materialism, and consumption. The relatively orderly behavior of generations of Americans at the bottom of the income distribution has been sustained by the belief that tomorrow would bring the blessings of wealth, if not for them, then for their children. Should the trend toward increasing societal wealth, sustained from the founding of the republic through the late 1970s, be drastically reversed by energy shortfall and the rising prices accompanying that condition, profound social unease might certainly be expected.

In an era of declining living standards, the cracks in the American social order may open into deep fissures. Not only will the poor come quickly to the realization that their lot is unlikely to improve, but the well-off will be faced by steady decrements in their own ability to achieve the benefits of material plenitude. In such a situation, what has been called the high "civil war potential" of American society will come into play. The meaning of life defined in terms of material gain, which each year becomes more unattainable to more people, may be seen as beyond hope or reason by the "decadent sensate society," as it has been called by Sorokin. Whether a "universal religion," as Toynbee identifies it, will emerge from the "decaying body social" of American materialism in decline is yet to be seen. Harman discerns clear signs of the emergence of such "societal transformation." Another possibility is that an unparalleled set of convulsions involving crime, general disorder, and random violence would immobilize society, inviting authoritarian rule and repression.

CENTRALIZING CONSEQUENCES OF SHORTFALL

The spatial impact of the scarcity of oil would be most directly felt in a radical decline in automobile transportation. The problems in assuring transportation in a time of energy shortfall appear to be far more difficult to solve than those accompanying the heating and cooling of space. Mass transportation is fueled by liquid combustibles, gasoline and oil, which are vulnerable to supply disruption and eventual exhaustion. The degree to which the electric car (assuming high energy-generating capacities by solar sources, especially photovoltaics and biomass fuel) can be developed is at present in question. We are not likely to be able to replace more than a fraction of the petroleum used for transportation by another fuel source. Thus, it would seem that transportation in the future will be based heavily on nonrenewable energy sources, which will be a factor encouraging the concentration of population and the reduction of lines of commutation to work, school, and play.

The spatial implications of energy available for transportation have been fully described by Fels and Munson, who have developed a set of scenarios interlinking patterns of transportation options and centralization-decentralization. These scenarios indicate that, at the extreme, our per capita energy consumption could vary between 14.7 and 151.2 thousand BTUs per day by the year 2000. The smaller figure applies to a scenario of "energy consciousness" in which people choose to live near where they work and to develop a social life that centers in those vicinities. The higher figure applies to a "luxury car" scenario in which big-car tastes continue to dominate and patterns of residential decentralization continue unabated.

The Fels and Munson study indicates that, by themselves, patterns of centralization or decentralization will make less of an impact on energy use than orientations pertaining to transportation use. Thus, a pattern of increasing land use centralization is seen to *facilitate* energy conservation, but not to *guarantee* it. Centralization is seen as a necessary condition for the five most conserving scenarios. Without centralization, the most conserving scenario uses nearly 70 thousand BTUs per person per day. With centralization, savings of as much as 75 percent of that figure can be achieved. Further, Fels and Munson demonstrate that the decision to seek energy conservation directly implies land use conservation. They identify their three lowest-energy-use scenarios as "non-viable" if land use patterns remain as dispersed as they presently are.

From the perspective of public policy advocacy, the case for reconcentration in response to transportation economies has been made in greatest detail by the Subcommittee on the City of the House Committee on Banking, Finance and Urban Affairs. Identifying "sprawl" as a "profligate waster of energy," the committee finds the travel commitments of the spread residential pattern at the heart of the matter: "The greatest energy waste due to sprawl stems from the greater distance people must travel . . . to work, to school, to shop, to eat out, to join friends, to attend meetings. All these extra miles mean extra energy."

The energy losses occasioned by sprawl may be reduced by seeing the city as "energy saver," the committee concludes. Walking, biking, and using public transport are all more common in the compact city than in areas of decentralized land use. "Because city residents walk and use mass transit, they use only half as much gasoline as nonurban residents. Commercial deliveries also consume less energy where consumers live closer to shopping nodes."

Compact cities allow energy saving by means of common walls and ceilings, heat islands, and wind buffers and provide opportunities for the development of cogeneration and district energy systems. These savings can be achieved not just in a few large cities, contends the committee, but in all communities, large and small, across the land. In a set of thirty detailed recommendations, the committee then proceeds to indicate how the tendency toward population decentralization can be reversed in a national commitment to the development of compactness.

The committee's focus on savings in personal transport as primary in generating compactness adds weight to the hypothesis that the most profound societal force impelling recentralization is the specter of oil shortfall. With such a development, the spatial pattern of our settlements would come to resemble Wurster's type of concentration and regional integration. In such a shortfall future:

1. What fuel there is available for transportation would be carefully allocated, with the highest priority being given to the transport of resources and the delivery of goods.
2. Workers would be strongly motivated to reside within walking or bicycling distances of their places of work. The development of "motel-type" housing would permit the maximum of worker mobility with the minimum of moving costs.
3. Personal transportation by fuel-powered vehicle would be substantially curtailed; wherever possible, communication would be conducted by telecommunications (including telephone). Pleasure travel would be drastically limited, particularly air travel, which would be largely limited to national defense.
4. The distribution of goods and services would be provided within subregional centers. So would, insofar as feasible, the production of goods and services.
5. No substantial increment of resources would be required for the construction of new urban places.

If these conditions were in force, settlement patterns might develop along the following lines:

1. Residential and economic patterns might center around a number (perhaps between 2,000 and 3,000) of regional nodes, within which most transportation, except that used for production, would be confined.
2. The most desirable housing within these subregional centers would be located within two kilometers of the node; other housing would be located within a ten kilometer radius of the node.
3. The locations of these nodes would emerge on the basis of current land use and occupy, in large part, existing shells. Criteria for node development would include:
   - High density of building space (residential, commercial, industrial) to land.
   - Proximity to circulation systems of an energy-poor society (rail lines for goods transport; interstate highways for goods transport; limited transport of persons by buses and automobiles).
4. Land outside the ten-kilometer radius of subregional nodes would be available for settlement only by farmers, self-sufficient nomads, and workers in the long-term vacation business. Included in this category would be a large portion of current suburban land, most existing towns with populations under 10,000, and almost all land in mountainous and rural areas.

Such a settlement pattern would obviously differ greatly from the present form and structure of the spread, or "corporate" city, as Gordon has called it. Least changed would be the middle-sized cities of the Northeast, already concentrated in land use. They would diversify their production, but would largely rely on existing shells. Larger cities and more greatly spread smaller cities would experience the development of multiple nodes within their present limits, each of which would take on an increasing autonomy. Most drastically affected would be the spread cities and most suburbs and small towns. Much of the land in these places would become largely depopulated since it falls outside the radius of the subregional nodes that would develop around present malls, apartment centers, suburban town centers, and other areas of potential concentration.

Almost all new construction would be contained within the nodes. House and land prices would skyrocket within the central ring in particular. Resettlement compensation would be required to assist those suburbanites whose real estate investments would be almost totally lost by the shifting residential patterns. Cultural experience would continue to be most accessible in those nodes that were formerly the central cities of great metropolises. These nodes would become the most highly valued places of residence in the new immobile urban world. In a curious paradox, the urban crisis would become resolved by suburban and exurban decline and abandonment.

Dudley Burton has developed a list of consequences for spatial settlements of the energy crisis:

- As energy costs rise relative to other costs (at least for a generation; with the maturation of photovoltaic technology or fusion power, they may go down), there will be tendencies toward increased urban density and concentration, though not in absolute size. That is, there will be an implosion of urban centers and an explosion in the number of cities.
- As energy costs rise, there will be an increasing substitution of communication for transportation. Electronic media of various sorts will flourish.
- As urban concentration increases, the car as the basic mode of transportation will be transformed and replaced. Both high- and low-technology options are likely: personalized, automated rapid transit systems on the one hand and bicycles on the other.
- As energy costs rise, the microstructure of cities—open space, parks, streets, and housing—will improve as a result of using building locations and landscaping to achieve natural air conditioning and energy conservation.
- As a result of migrations and new development patterns, there will be a variety of urban experiments ranging from homesteading of abandoned central city buildings and the construction of new towns like Columbia, Maryland, to the design of self-sufficient communities such as the ARK (Nova Scotia), Arcosanti (Paolo Soleri's Arizona Community), and Serro Gordo, Oregon.

In the event of a future disruption of oil, occasioned perhaps by a revolution in Saudi Arabia, a prolonged regional war in the Persian Gulf, or a set of concatenate calamities as sketched by Vacca, the United States might find itself facing an immediate shortfall of one-half or more of its daily oil diet. If military mobilization is chosen in such a situation, domestic oil supplies might fall even more precipitously.

Should this shortfall scenario descend while the vast proportion of U.S. buildings and homes remains dependent on nonrenewable fuel for heating and cooling, the magnitude of disruption of daily life would be enormous. The most severe rationing of fuel would not, under such circumstances, allow for the provision of adequate fuel to heat our homes, fuel our factories, and provide our work force with the mobility to complete its normal commutation.

Within months, as the recognition emerged that the shortfall would be prolonged, residential patterns would begin to shift as individuals and families sought to minimize daily travel. Mass transit would become saturated at peak hours, and membership in a car pool with assured gasoline supply would become a mark of privilege. Many individuals and families would seek to double up in residences with friends or relatives, as now occurs in recessionary periods. House exchanges would be proposed, and some would become permanent as they met the needs of both parties for greater access to the work place.

If a shortfall was caused by a war of several years' duration, we would find our daily lives greatly altered. Without solar heating in place in the majority of homes, living space per person would be reduced greatly. New, economizing life styles reminiscent of Third World experiences would likely emerge.

University of California urbanist Richard L. Meier has described the process in great detail. He asks about New York: Would it "be able to function after an extended coal strike, or a serious flareup of the Arab wars? Undoubtedly gasoline would have to be rationed, thermostats turned down to 10°C (50°F), surplus rooms closed off, the hot water turned to tepid, and everyone would wear one or two layers more of clothing."

What would life be like after three years of such shortfall? Meier continues: "Experience suggests that water-using services, like bottle-washing, would shut down, and pressure in the pipes would be maintained only part of the day, being restored only for firefighting during the period shut down—as in Bombay before the monsoon. People would fill bathtubs, barrels, and buckets to tide them over" the waterless times. Such a form of urbanism, Meier notes, is not unlike the situation in turn-of-the-century New York, when the parlor was rarely heated even in the dead of winter.

Meier believes that much may be learned from the Third World in the way of reorienting urban transportation in case of energy shortfall. He notes that a "bus station needs to be as carefully designed as an airport and will require redesign as frequently. Scarce land and expensive human time can also be conserved by encouraging round-the-clock operation of services and industrial estates. Singapore is now the best model for distributing activities round-the-clock, and it will become even more efficient when it is able to make full use of world market situations transmitted to it through communication satellites."

No matter how ingeniously arguments such as Meier's are presented regarding the viability of the energy-short city, the stark fact remains that these images are unthinkable to many and distasteful to almost all Americans. Note the combination of the themes of unthinkability and distastefulness in a *Business Week* review:

> Mankind has never willingly given up the fruits of technological progress. . . . Totally unexpected technological change can occur in the future, as it has in the past, to make today's predictions of disaster seem absurd. . . . We will continue to rely on new technology to solve the problems that our present technology causes. Given the opportunity to be mobile, with an automobile, for example, people will not voluntarily return to walking. This challenges the auto industry—or perhaps the bicycle industry—to develop a vehicle that people can afford to operate when gasoline is $10 or $20 a gal.

Its undesirability notwithstanding, it appears that we are vulnerable to the shortfall possibility, with all its dislocations and discomforts, so long as we remain dependent upon nonrenewable energy sources for the overwhelming proportion of our uses. Once we have moved to the point that the preponderance of reliance has switched to solar energy, our vulnerability to war, strike, embargo, sabotage, and accident will have been substantially reduced.

The transition to a renewable energy base can be accomplished in a variety of ways, ranging from those that are highly orderly to those that are largely unplanned and disorderly. If we wait to develop renewable sources until we are in the throes of a severe interruption of energy supplies, we shall scramble for the addition of rooftop collectors, insulation, and industrial solar-generation equipment in a way that will overtax production and give little hope of maintaining levels of energy sufficiency, at least through the period of crisis conversion. If, on the other hand, we set about with foresight to prepare for future disruptions in energy supply and price, a greatly different spatial future may be ours to choose.

DECENTRALIZING CONSEQUENCES OF SHORTFALL

Not all predictions of life under energy shortfall involve spatial centralization. Visions of "urban reimplosion," of a return to the walking city of the eighteenth century and before (enhanced by modern telecommunications, of course), have been challenged by the studies of Dale Keyes, who reports that "savings in annual energy consumption made possible by accommodating new growth more efficiently would be around 0.35 percent of the national total. This is obviously not an overwhelmingly large saving." In a like vein, David Crane finds that requiring 20 percent greater fuel efficiency for cars and 50 percent greater heating and cooling efficiency for new buildings would reduce the amount of additional energy required by 1985 from an increment of 50 percent to 44 percent above 1976 levels.

Keyes takes the position that the future will build incrementally on the present and that spatial change will not be drastic:

> In sum, my view of the fuel-scarce city underscores the strength of forces currently shaping our metropolitan areas. The fuel-scarce city and its environs will have smaller populations and centripetal forces will continue to dominate the overall pattern of development. Employment, which is largely insensitive to increases in the price of energy, will continue to decentralize. Most households with children will maintain their distaste for inner-city living but will favor suburban locations closer to where they work. . . . New residential as well as commercial developments will appear even more frequently near highway interchanges and transit stops. Per capita travel within the metropolitan area will decline somewhat; but autos, still the choice of the vast majority of travelers, will perform their task much more efficiently. Electric cars will be common. Alternative energy sources for on-site use will have gone beyond the experimental stage, with whole subdivisions and clustered homes in planned developments fueled by synthetic gas and solar energy.

Other statements have been made to the point that energy shortfall contains within it a set of implications more conducive to decentralization than to reconcentration. Peterson and Hempel have analyzed the decentralizing influence of solar, recycling, and communications technologies and note that "each of these technological developments offers an individual the opportunity to withdraw from traditional dependency relationships which have been created by the basic urban institutions of our time: city governments, utility companies, major educational centers and the workplaces of corporate capitalism. . . . There is increasing evidence that dispersed settlement patterns can be combined with what we have previously considered 'urban' levels of quality of life." The settlement future described by Peterson and Hempel is one of "low-density citiness," a phenomenon lucidly analyzed by Bradshaw and Blakely.

Clearly, as will be discussed more fully in the following chapter, the solar thrust contains within it strong decentralizing forces. Insofar as it is directed to the personal collection of solar energy and the household production of at least a portion of food, its decentralizing tendencies are paramount. As Sim Van der Ryn has noted, the typical half-acre suburban plot is ideally suited to the collection and recycling of solar use, as well as to the growing of a significant proportion of family food needs.

Dudley Burton has also discussed the decentralizing possibilities of a future based on renewable energy. He notes the importance of the movement back to rural communities or small towns "to capture elements of both lifestyles and alternative energy supply. Examples of lifestyle effects include small or semiindustrial operations which avoid some of the anomie of mass industrialization. The alternative energy supply would include a return to the use in some areas of wood for home heating, the revival of backyard gardening, and access to solar energy."

Burton does not see this movement as more than marginal at present, but sees it as an increasing possibility in years ahead. Others, faced with the plausibility of both the reconcentration and dispersion positions, have chosen to conclude that little change in spatial patterns is to be expected. A United Nations seminar concluded that the centralization path would emerge only in a "minimum disturbance" scenario, in which energy decisions were deferred in order to gain greater perspective, and that three other scenarios would generate little shift in spatial form. Similarly, *The New York Times,* in its forecast for the 1980s, envisioned little shift between Frostbelt and Sunbelt as the decade advanced.

The perspectives of those who have studied the impact of energy choices on urban futures are clearly affected by the patterns by which energy is seen to change, both in supply and form. Those who envisage energy shortfall describe a future in which continuing reliance is placed on unrenewable energy sources and these sources become subject to rapid price increases and selective interruptions of supply, eventuating in a situation in which they are not available in sufficient quantities to fulfill the needs of commerce, heating, and transit. On the other hand, those who envisage a rapid transformation to reliance on renewable energy sources describe a future in which energy opulence becomes energy sufficiency and neither price escalation nor supply interruption becomes a systematic, social, or economic problem.

The intellectual bases of these two perspectives may be more fully understood if the variety of choices of urban form are systematically discussed in tandem with the varieties of energy forms.

CENTRALIZATION AND DECENTRALIZATION IN OUR ENERGY FUTURE

Energy-related factors may encourage both centralization and decentralization. The sudden and prolonged unavailability of petroleum, consumer choices to minimize oil use in response to price rises, and the clustering of buildings to achieve economies in joint wall, ceiling, and floor use, for example, all imply centralization. On the other hand, the desire to collect solar energy by rooftop or land-sited collectors, the growing of food at home, and the development of isolated and autonomous communities all imply a decentralized pattern of land use.

James Zucchetto has reviewed over twenty studies that seek to predict the spatial implications of energy shortfall or price increases. He finds that these studies are nearly evenly divided between those predicting increased concentration and those predicting increased decentralization.

Those who predict increased concentration, Zucchetto writes, share the view that "dispersed settlement patterns have been made possible . . . by the availability of a modern road network system, the private automobile, and abundant supplies of inexpensive gasoline." These authors see a concentration of spatial patterns resulting from the need to reduce transportation costs in a time of shortfall and from the greater energy efficiency of the medium-sized multifamily urban dwelling.

Those who foresee increased decentralization, on the other hand, note that the minimal fuel savings a family might achieve in moving from the suburb to the city would not, in most cases, compensate for moving costs and the loss of accustomed suburban amenities. These authors see many firms moving to suburban nodes and economic growth concentrating in smaller towns rather than cities. The decentralizing perspective, with which Zucchetto identifies himself, foresees "a decline in very large urban places, a development of small places about nodes of the transportation network." The locational advantages of the Sunbelt over the Frostbelt and the decline in urban economic advantage in an age of telecommunications further contributes to the likelihood of decentralization, Zucchetto asserts.

That we must choose between centralization and decentralization in a time of energy shortfall and transformation is an assumption, and one that may be questioned. As George Homans has warned, we moderns face the peril of impaling ourselves on the horns of many a false dilemma.

If we consider the four energy configurations developed earlier in this chapter with Wurster's four spatial patterns, some of the variability of our energy future may be explained (see Table 5.2). The table suggests that each urban form draws support from a different pattern of energy forms. Present trends in spatial form and structure are supportable only by the development of renewable energy sources, for a reliance on nonrenewable sources for primary support forces the choice of the diversified-integrated model. The general-dispersion model, on the other hand, could be supported only by a reliance on renewable solar energy and that in a problematic fashion, as will be discussed below. The concentrated supercity fits only with a renewable nuclear-fuel and energy-rich future. And the diversified-integrated pattern fits each energy form, supporting the contention that it is the safest bet as we approach the uncertain future of energy forms and structures.

A review of the evidence for each of these contentions follows.

1. A primary reliance on nonrenewable energy forms cannot sustain any urban form but the diversified-integrated model because the three principal sources of nonrenewable energy are subject to clear limits of expansion. Oil is running out, worldwide, and will be subject to increased price inflation and uncertainty of supply throughout this century, its twenty-first century remainder likely to be perceived as a precious mineral to be employed only for selected industrial applications. Coal is limited for the production of electricity because of the pollution it causes as well as the difficulty with which its mining rate can be accelerated. And nonrenewable forms of nuclear generation will continue to be bedeviled by the legacy of Three Mile Island (particularly the increasing unattractiveness as an economic investment), problems of disposal, and terrorist threat. It now appears likely that few new nuclear-power installations of the nonrenewable type will ever be built and that those on line will simply be permanently shut down as they expire. Most are likely to be out of commission by the last decade of this century. Thus, the energy path of nonrenewable nuclear fuel appears to be conducive only to a low-transportation, low-energy future—one that can only be sustained, with some substantial discomfort, by the multinucleated urbanized form Wurster called "diversified-integrated." As Lovins notes, "Centralized energy sources encourage industrial clustering and urbanization."

2. The other hard-energy path, renewable nuclear power, might

Table 5.2

Interrelating Spatial and Energy Forms

If primary reliance is placed ———→ then ———→ the likelihood of **SPATIAL FORMS** is:
on these ENERGY FORMS

SPATIAL FORMS

ENERGY FORMS	I. Present Trends	II. General Dispersion	III. Supercity	IV. Diversified-Integrated
I. Nonrenewable Coal, Gas, Nuclear Energy	−	−	−	+
II. Nonrenewable Oil	−	−	−	+
III. Renewable Nuclear Energy	?	−	+	+
IV. Renewable Solar Energy	+	?	−	+

+ Congenial pattern for primary support   − Uncongenial pattern for primary support
? Uncertain pattern for primary support

Source: Adapted from the author's "Forms and Structure of Spatial Patterns and Distribution," in Energy Resources and Conservation Related to Built Environment (Pergamon Press, 1980), pp. 145-160. Reprinted with permission from Pergamon Press.

sustain two of the four spatial forms. Renewable nuclear power is a centralized energy source that favors centralized locational tendencies. Indeed, the spatial form most congenial to an energy-rich renewable-nuclear-fuel future would likely be the concentrated supercity, with its limited needs for automobile transportation and its huge energy needs for construction. This path is not likely to generate sufficient electricity to sustain either present trends or a pattern of general dispersion, unless accompanied by a determined program of energy conservation.

Centralized residential patterns would minimize transmission costs of nuclear-powered electricity, but would also maximize citizen anxiety and insecurity regarding the safety of large nuclear installations. The diversified-integrated model, providing a modicum of spatial insulation from centralized plants at the cost of increased prices for transmission and lessened transportation access to urban amenities might be preferred by many citizens.

3. Choice of the path of renewable solar-energy permits at least as large a choice of spatial forms as the hypothetical path of renewable nuclear-energy. The solar-energy future would eliminate with certainty only the concentrated supercity. Many present patterns could be sustained by determined efforts of conservation, solar retrofitting, and reservation of the use of liquid fuels for the powering of automobiles, trucks, and airplanes. The path of renewable solar-energy accommodates most congenially the diversified-integrated city built on the ideological base of "sufficiency but not waste."

The range of spatial options in a future of renewable energy, then, appears to be broader and less constrained than the range in a future using nonrenewable energy sources. To be sure, the maximization of solar energy will require a good deal of space for the array of solar cells, water heaters, windmills, and small hydrogenerators that will collect much of the solar energy. Further, a society that seeks to maximize solar use will still require a well-maintained conventional power system as backup for use at night and on cloudy days. Nevertheless, as will be seen in the next chapter, such spatial uses are viewed as congenial to urban densities in many contemporary studies.

Simply because a particular choice of energy options gives rise to a wider range of spatial patterns is, of course, not a sufficient reason to argue for the superiority of that choice. Nor is the centralization versus decentralization question the only one that may be asked about the future of settlement patterns. Indeed, it may be that the argument over centralizing and decentralizing forces will not prove to be the most important one about the spatial implications of energy choices. It may simply prove to be the first question to which urbanists gave their attention when they began seriously to probe the impact of energy shortfall.

As we seek to understand the future form of U.S. spatial patterns, other questions will be asked as well: Why will we come to live in different settlement patterns? How will our places of work and residence be placed across the continental space of the United States? Why will some of us reside in cities, others in suburbs, and still others in towns and rural areas?

Surely it is the mosaic of our future patterns of community and land use that is of most interest to us, and not simply the question of the fate of the theory of expanding scale. It is to these patterns that our attention turns in the following chapter.

6

Emerging Spatial Patterns for Cities and Towns

To understand the ways in which the mosaic of the American community may come to be pieced together in the years ahead, it will be useful to develop a model of the spatial structure of communities. Such a model, a relatively simple one, will be presented in this chapter. This model links the three societal scenarios developed earlier in this book to the ways and places in which Americans will come to live in the years ahead.

From the three scenarios developed in Chapters 2 and 3—Good Luck, Continuity, and Hard Luck—four elements will be highlighted in the model. These societal elements most directly affect the ways people live: energy, communications, economics, and life style.

DETERMINANTS OF SPATIAL USE

Energy, the first independent factor, has been shown to shape spatial patterns through its availability for industrial use, commercial- and residential-space heating and cooling, and personal transportation. Chapters 4 and 5 have explored in detail the ways in which changing patterns of energy availability and pricing might affect residential choice.

Communications, the second independent factor, affects spatial patterns because of the necessity for persons to interact in order to advance a wide variety of personal and economic interests. Without face-to-face communication, such forms of community life as urban neighborhoods and concentrated commercial centers would not exist. Similarly, small towns and regional markets have developed to facilitate the communication necessary for many social and economic transactions.

Contemporary developments in communications technology, however, are proceeding at a dizzying pace. The innovations give rise to advances that facilitate communication without requiring face-to-face interaction. Thus, the development of the computer and the advances generated by the microprocessor have created an "information revolution" that permits communication by persons who need not move from their computer or telephone. Such developments reduce enormously the amount of energy required for communication.

Economics, the third independent factor, affects spatial patterns because of the necessity to organize and perform work in such facilities as factories, stores, and service centers (such as schools or hospitals). Bringing large numbers of people together with machines and resources for production has been the primary economic characteristic of the industrial era. Production has also affected spatial patterns. Those who own or control processes of production have usually received a far greater bounty of income and wealth than those who are employed in the actual processes of production, and money affects where one can afford to live.

Life style is the fourth factor that critically affects spatial patterns. The United States is a consumer society in which individuals seek to acquire a mix of material possessions that maximizes their own approximation to the "good life." For most Americans, their most important possession is their house. The location of that house has been central to its worth and the satisfaction provided by it.

In the years following World War II, the address of distinction was located in the middle-class suburban belt that grew around central cities. In recent years, the quest has become increasingly focused on climate and access to outdoor recreation. In both periods, with the exception of small countermovements of gentrification or reurbanization in some cities, the quest for amenity has led away from the city. Indeed, in its contemporary manifestations, the values that are sought are those of the small community, privacy, a parcel of land, access to natural scenery, and participation in the "good life." In many cases, these preferences have led Americans away from the urban Northeast to the sprawling acreage of the South, Southwest, and West—the Sunbelt.

A MODEL OF SPATIAL FUTURES

The independent factors are seen in the model as producing different configurations of class, community, and region. To see how this is effected, it will be necessary to identify a number of different lines along which each of the independent factors may develop. We have already done this for energy in Chapter 2 where four different futures were developed: the Good Luck positions of energy plenitude and solar transition, the Continuity position of incremental energy transition, and the Hard Luck possibility of energy shortfall.

Similarly, we have identified for the communications factor positions that vary with the speed and pervasiveness of developments in this field. One position we called "continuing development" of communications; an even faster pace of development gives rise to a "communications revolution."

On the economic dimension, three major possibilities emerge from the earlier discussion: the Good Luck possibility of economic growth and recovery, the Continuity future of continued stagflation, and the Hard Luck position of economic decline. Economic growth and recovery is the Reagan scenario transcendent: inflation and unemployment reduced, productivity rising, national wealth increasing. Continued stagflation is the projection of the trends of the late 1970s into the foreseeable future: low growth, high inflation, high but not intolerable unemployment. Economic decline is the Hard Luck scenario: raging inflation, high unemployment, impending worldwide depression, and economic collapse.

In relation to life style, we can identify positions of "intensified quest," "restrained quest," and "transformation." Intensified quest means the triumph of me-generation privatism and untrammeled interpersonal competition, the Hard Luck possibility. Restrained quest implies a continuing and unresolved struggle between the forces of individualism and transformation, the Continuity future. Transformation means the widespread adoption of "new-age" values of ecological rootedness and collective concern, the emergence of the Good Luck position.

What the model seeks to explain is who will live how and where. This means that it has as its outcome variables of socioeconomic class, community type, and region.

Socioeconomic class is most often analyzed by social scientists in terms of five categories: upper, upper middle, lower middle, working, and lower. Upper-class persons possess substantial wealth and adequate income. Upper-middle-class individuals are professionals; they possess moderate wealth and comfortable incomes. Lower-middle-class persons typically fill clerical and sales positions; their incomes are modest and they own little more than their homes and automobiles. Working-class persons work in the direct production of goods; their wealth is limited and their incomes range from low to nearly comfortable. Finally, lower-class individuals are unemployed, underemployed, or engaged in manual labor of low reward; they have little or no earned income and their wealth is most often negative. That is, they owe more than they own.

Members of the classes are not evenly distributed among the major community types in the United States: cities, suburbs, towns, and rural areas. A somewhat higher proportion of working-class and lower-class persons resides in cities than in suburbs. Suburban populations, to the contrary, overrepresent members of the upper-middle class, while lower-middle-class persons are rather equally distributed between city and suburb. Towns and rural areas, on the other hand, tend to host higher concentrations of lower-middle-class and working-class persons.

A third way of looking at the population of the United States is in terms of region. Just as each individual may be placed in a community type, so may each community be located in a region. For the purposes of our model, a distinction will be drawn between the two major American regions: Frostbelt and Sunbelt. The Sunbelt will be considered as the Southern, Southwestern, and Western states. The Frostbelt is identified as the Northeastern, North Central, and Great Plains states.

The four factors may be combined in myriad ways: The energy factor has four possible positions, two other factors have three possibilities, and there are two communications positions. This means that the four factors give rise to seventy-two configurations of possible futures. These numbers may be greatly reduced by limiting the options for each factor to those suggested by the Good Luck, Continuity, and Hard Luck scenarios.

Presenting these options schematically (Fig. 6.1), we see that four elements—energy, communications, economics, and life style—of the future emerge in the context of three scenarios: Hard Luck, Continuity, and Good Luck, and thereby affect the shape of socioeconomic class in community types and regions.

SPATIAL SCENARIOS

The Continuity scenario projects a future, not surprisingly, that resembles the recent past. American society remains troubled by recurrent inflationary price shocks in energy, as well as occasional interruptions in supply. Stagflation and cultural confusion continue to characterize an era of malaise.

Socioeconomically, the Continuity scenario predicts small losses in well-being and real income for almost all Americans. Only the rich avoid an erosion in economic power; the persons at the bottom lose

Figure 6.1

Spatial Implications of Four Societal Scenarios

SCENARIOS	Imply	SPATIAL CONSEQUENCES
<u>Good Luck Scenario,</u> <u>First Possibility</u>		
Energy plenitude Communications revolution Economic recovery Restrained quest life-style	⟹	Enhanced well-being □ of all classes □ in all communities □ in all regions
<u>Good Luck Scenario,</u> <u>Second Possibility</u>		
Solar transition Communications revolution Economic recovery Life-style transformation	⟹	Enhanced well-being and increasing equality □ of all classes □ in all communities □ in all regions
<u>Continuity Scenario</u>		
Incremental energy transition Continuing communications development Continued stagflation Restrained quest life-style	⟹	Small losses in well-being □ for most Americans, particularly those in lower and working classes □ especially in cities □ particularly in the Frost Belt
<u>Hard Luck Scenario</u>		
Energy shortfall Continuing communications development Economic decline Intensified quest life-style	⟹	Large losses in well-being □ for all groups, including the rich □ in cities, towns, and suburbs □ especially in the Frost Belt

the most. Squeezed by the political wrath of the lower-middle and middle classes, who see their visions of affluence fading, persons at the bottom of the economic structure have neither jobs nor adequate income.

In such a future, population shifts rapidly toward the Sunbelt, lured by access to renewable and nonrenewable energy, employment in flourishing communications industries, and visions of moderate climate, dramatic scenery, and the "good life."

The decline of the Northeastern and North Central cities continues in this scenario, and the urban crisis also begins to invade the suburbs in these areas. Many of the most able in the work force are enticed to Sunbelt positions. Housing markets are slow; public services, such as education and transportation, decline as taxes increase; rates of industrial closing and disinvestment increase. The center of national wealth and power decisively moves from the great metropolitan complexes of New York, Detroit, Chicago, and Boston to the new capitals of Los Angeles, Houston, Dallas, and Phoenix.

The Hard Luck scenario intensifies many of the trends already under way. In this future, the Frostbelt city becomes the home of an ever-larger population of deprived and desperate individuals and families. These urban ranks are swelled by former members of the working and middle classes who find themselves unwilling draftees in the war on inflation. The few persons of high income who remain in the cities seek to defend their neighborhoods or high-rise towers from ravages of increasing urban crime and violence. Numerous cities abandon their systems of public transit, as Birmingham did temporarily in 1981. Public school systems begin to close in Frostbelt cities in the mid-1980s, and organized rebellion begins to emerge in some cities.

The suburbs of the Frostbelt become the refuge for many middle-class urbanites who are able to escape the reach of disorder and declining public service. But their housing aspirations exceed their ability to pay, and many suffer real losses in housing quality as they seek to escape the city's reach. The deregulation of natural gas prices in 1985 leads many suburban families to the brink of foreclosure. Their lines of communication, as well, become stretched beyond the comfort of family stability, especially in the increasingly prevalent two-career family.

A strong market develops in the city for returning middle-class families, desperate for inexpensive housing closer to their places of work. Seeking to save on both their energy bills and their mortgage payments, these prospective residents organize collectively to pressure city mayors for adequate services as a condition for their migration. Faced with the opportunity to increase the tax base of the city with more employed residents and faced with the threat from commercial and corporate firms to move to the suburbs, the mayors of large cities turn to policies that result in the expulsion of the poor. One-way bus tickets to Sunbelt cities are provided by welfare agencies to the unemployed and their families, low-income housing that does not meet code standards is demolished, and income maintenance programs discontinued by the federal government are not replaced at the local level. State legislation facilitating the construction of state-funded housing for the unemployed on the edges of metropolitan areas is vigorously supported in the 1990s by the big-city mayors, most of whom are black.

Meanwhile, in the Sunbelt, a higher level of prosperity is maintained as increasing military expenditures provide for sustained economic growth. Concern rises about the possibility of an influx of unemployed Frostbelt families, and high barriers to migrants are erected in the form of five-year residency requirements for the receipt of any public service save preventive health care and public education.

In the Good Luck scenario envisioned by President Reagan and his administration, a rosy picture is presented. If a reasonably smooth energy transition is effected, this scenario projects immediate gains for persons of greater means. These gains then trickle swiftly to persons at lower points in the class structure. Suburbs and towns are particularly advantaged in this scenario, as they house the bulk of the middle- and upper-class families. A substantial bias in favor of the Sunbelt may also be detected. However attractive this vision of America's future might appear, it seems a long shot at best.

Another Good Luck scenario also seems unlikely, but appears to rest on a stronger reality base than the Reagan vision of a recaptured Golden Age. This scenario is based on the successful transformation to an energy base of conservation and renewable resources. As a shortfall scenario, it posits successful adaptation to rising prices of gas, oil, and nuclear energy. This scenario has been extensively developed by the Friends of the Earth. Unlike the previous visions, it does not necessarily lead to increasing inequality and continuing Sunbelt advantage. Rather, it assumes that we shall, for the most part, stay where we are and create more satisfactory life ways in the various communities in which we live.

The Friends of the Earth have developed a detailed image of life in the year 2050. They anticipate that most Americans will at that time be living in communities with populations between 50,000 and 200,000. Great cities will have become subdivided into small communities, which can provide jobs, education, and recreation. The Friends of the Earth ascribe these spatial patterns to a "simultaneous implosion and explosion of population. The implosion would occur as the automobile was abandoned as the primary means of city transit. The explosion would come about with the reestablishment of distinct – as opposed to megalopolitan – urban areas of reduced size. These areas would generally contain 200,000 or fewer residents, a

population still manageable in terms of the economics of city operation, full pedestrian and bicycle access to all districts, and accessibili-
ty to surrounding food-producing lands."

The Friends of the Earth hypothesize that these urban entities will
come about through a combination of legislation and individual
residential choices. Within existing cities with populations far greater
than 200,000, they envision the development of urban agriculture:

> In slum neighborhoods out of necessity, in better-off neighborhoods
> out of frugality or civic pride, these vacant areas could be converted
> into community gardens and orchards. The cities, straining under the
> loss of tax base as a result of out-migration, would welcome this use of
> empty lots. After a time, the trend of building rehabilitation, urban
> open-space accrual, and new building would lead to multi-nucleated
> patterns of compact towns and communities on the sites of present-day
> megalopoli. Such planned development, with appropriate zoning or-
> dinances, would integrate the energy, agricultural, transport, and
> recreational needs of a community while avoiding unnecessary
> transportation of food and materials from distant regions. Zoning in cer-
> tain areas would allow a mix of commercial and residential uses of the
> same block, and in the same building complex, so residents would
> need to travel only short distances to shop and to their place of work.

Thus, conclude the Friends of the Earth, "we envision recent
trends, with encouragement and structuring from the legislation,
leading to a restructuring of settlements." Similarly, Leven and his
associates have viewed the multinucleated city as the most likely
form into which the "mature metropolis" will emerge as its population
shrinks and resource patterns change. In such a metropolis, residential and economic patterns emerge around regional nodes, within
which most economic, social, and recreational life is confined for
residents.

The image of a spatial future that will best suit the needs of a solar-
energy future that is short of fossil fuel thus begins to take clear and
concrete form. At the core of our present metropolitan cities, open
land is increasingly created and cultivated, while existing urban
homes become fully weatherized, highly equipped with solar collectors, and well fitted for water and other resource conservation. Urban neighborhoods become increasingly self-contained, and lines of
commutation shorten as increasing numbers of workers find positions in their own part of the city or relocate closer to existing
employment. As the Friends of the Earth put it, "As private transportation becomes more and more costly, and as local grocers, butchers,

bakers, druggists, jewelers, booksellers, restauranters [sic], and clothiers are able to supply most of local residents' needs, the neighborhood and the town would regain their social and community functions."

In the suburbs, a similar process of clustering around urban nodes is to be expected. The new neighborhood cities of suburbia would experience an intensification of their land use, particularly near the centers of nodal development. The Friends of the Earth state: "It may be that the parking lots of today's shopping centers will be the sites of tomorrow's housing."

Sim Van der Ryn describes the advantages suburban communities possess in the move to a multinucleated urban future: "The prevalent suburban pattern in the United States could easily be adopted to save even more energy (than present urban areas) by being converted to intensive garden production." One such project indicates that a plot of one-tenth of an acre could produce up to $20,000 worth of vegetables per year, if one person worked a forty-hour week eight months a year. "The 19 million acres of suburban lawns in this country are major consumers of pesticides and fertilizers; if they were converted to mini-farms, they could . . . feed this country."

Within the spread urban areas of the South and West and many other suburban areas, "removing redundant streets would add many millions more of farmable acres. . . . Most of our cities are built on flat, alluvial plains, and the soil is often the best there is." Space is also plentiful for solar collectors in suburban areas. So long as the residents are willing to live near their places of employment, it would appear that the suburban habitat is well suited to the solar-energy future.

As for small towns and rural areas, the multinucleated vision anticipates population growth in those areas that develop viable nodes and population decline for the communities left in isolation by increasing costs of transportation. The isolated farms and ranches of the Western states will surely require energy assistance if they are to retain both their viability and their access to urban America in the solar-energy future.

Finally, enormous expanses of land will continue to lie beyond the boundaries of the nodes of today's urban neighborhoods, concentrated suburbs, chosen small towns, and surviving farms and ranches. Americans who will choose to live self-sufficient lives may live in these areas beyond the range of the reconcentrated yet decentralized centers of population.

The availability of solar-energy advantages in both city and suburb will channel future development in both Frostbelt and Sunbelt areas. The Northeastern and North Central states are likely to capitalize on the strengths of their compact cities—lower energy needs for transportation, shared walls, and established mass transit. Their suburbs are likely to become more urban in appearance as the multinucleated metropolis takes form. Southern and Western cities will likewise maximize their chief energy assets—bounteous solar access and lower space-heating needs. Their cities and suburbs are likely to remain relatively indistinguishable, though the multi-nucleated form will become increasingly defined as a response to dwindling transportation capacity.

The transformation of life styles and spatial patterns to a solar-energy future may be orderly or traumatic, depending on the severity of hard-path disruption and the development of our societal foresight. Obviously, an orderly transition would be preferable.

AN ORDERLY TRANSITION TO SOLAR ENERGY

Our national vulnerability to energy disruption is apparent. Equally evident is our capacity to soften the impact of such disruption by an orderly transition to renewable energy sources. In such a transition, national energy policy would encourage and enable the development of renewable resources to the maximum feasible extent for purposes of heating and cooling buildings, fueling industry, and transporting people and goods. At the same time, vigorous efforts to reduce energy use would continue by encouraging conservation and promoting new systems of efficient energy use.

The process of solar conversion will surely continue to receive greatest focus in the area of heating and cooling space. Here, our present technology is capable of meeting an extraordinary proportion of our national use and need. By carefully weatherizing a home—adding insulation, installing weather stripping, caulking window frames, and installing storm windows and doors—the average owner of a house or an apartment may achieve 20 to 25 percent reductions in energy use. By combining such weatherization with a reduction in room temperatures, savings may be increased to 40 percent. If, on top of these savings (and usually on top of the house), a solar collector is installed, the savings may rise to as high as 60 to 80 percent, depending on region and house location.

These savings, substantial as they are, may be only the beginning on the road to self-sufficiency in heating and cooling. Each year between 2 and 3 percent of our national housing stock is replaced. If each of these new homes were built according to well-established principles of passive solar design, known since classical times, our housing stock would require substantially less energy for heating and cooling by the year 2000, perhaps by an order of 20 percent.

Advances in solar technology are expected in the years ahead. Generation of electricity by photovoltaic-cell collection, a space technology, is expected to be attractively priced for widespread application in the late 1980s. If electricity can be generated from rooftop collectors at a reasonable cost, home owners will be able to generate not only sufficient electricity to heat and cool their weatherized homes, but also significant amounts of excess power. Under the Public Utilities Regulatory Policies Act of 1978, the electrical grid system presently used by utility companies to distribute power is open to access by producers of electricity other than utility companies. Cooperatives and even individuals producing electricity from their own wind or photovoltaic systems are able to sell the energy they generate, but do not immediately use, to the regional grid. These producing consumers will purchase electricity at times when their homes consume more energy than their systems generate.

The coming emergence of the household as a producer of energy not only will thoroughly revise relations between utility companies and consumers, but also will create a widely dispersed cottage industry, the generation of electrical power. David Morris notes that the General Electric Corporation is developing a rooftop shingle that contains a hexagonal photovoltaic cell. When the cost of roofing one's home with such shingles drops to $15,000, many Americans will become producers of energy.

Photovoltaic power has the potential of greatly easing the impact of hard-path discontinuity. In addition to heating and cooling space, photovoltaic power can be used by individual home and land owners to generate electricity for their own transport, by battery-powered electric automobiles or motorcycles.

Small wonder that many students of solar futures have concluded that spatial deconcentration will be the way of the future. If sufficient solar energy can be generated from rooftops to heat and cool our homes, and more, why, these observers ask, should not people choose to live self-sufficient lives in the area of food production as well? The decentralizing imperative of the solar future is perhaps most starkly drawn by Jeremy Rifkin, who foresees a "massive shift of people away from the cities and back to the farms" to engage in "small-scale labor-intensive agriculture."

Cities will not entirely disappear, Rifkin predicts, but will be scaled down to "their preindustrial size of 50,000 to 100,000 citizens." Transportation and industrial activity will also be scaled down to meet the reduced energy needs and supplies of "low entropy" society. Rifkin does not provide any explanation of how the new farmers will link into broader societal institutions, nor does he discuss how large cities will "scale down" to preindustrial population levels.

On the limits of solar generation, however, Rifkin's argument is telling: "The use of solar energy cannot be divorced from the stock of fixed terrestrial matter that it interacts on and converts. In living and in industrial processes, solar energy must always be combined with other terrestrial resources in order to produce a product. That conversion process always results in the further dissipation of the fixed stock of terrestrial resources on the planet." To put it bluntly: "A solar infrastructure derived from and dependent on nonrenewable resources cannot be supported on a scale necessary to maintain highly industrialized economies. The nonrenewable resources will simply not be available in the quantities required." There is no escape from the dissipation of energy in the solar future, Rifkin suggests. Entropy will still limit our growth and threaten our industrial way of life.

Even under the most beneficial scenarios that one might construct of the photovoltaic future, strong pressures to decentralize will remain. If it is profitable to install cells on one's roof, it will be more profitable to collect sunlight on some acreage out back as well. If it is desirable to live in close-knit communities, it will be most desirable to share in activities that require land, such as collective food production, as well as to create boundaries that assure the spatial integrity of the group. If it becomes increasingly possible to work at home from one's computer, then why not choose the path of increasing scale that has been the ancient aspiration of so many Americans?

There is no doubt that forces of profit, communal living, and (paradoxically, perhaps) isolationism will continue to affect Americans—and that decentralization will remain a preferred option of many whenever feasible. But it is also true that decentralization implies the need for physical mobility, and that mobility remains endangered even in the sunniest solar future.

Solar energy can fuel personal transport in two major ways: by alcohol and by battery-stored electricity. In neither case do the benefits of decentralizing production appear to compensate for the costs associated with extending lines of personal transportation. To be sure, if individuals were willing to move to remote locations and remain there in relative immobility, the incremental energy they might grow and process through grain alcohol, or collect by photovoltaic cells, would surely exceed what they would use to fuel their automobiles, however propelled. But this sedentary decentralized future does not seem likely, unless compelled by external adversity. Contemporary Americans, though they often state preferences for decentralized spatial patterns, are also insistent on access to automobiles and airplanes for keeping in touch with friends, family, cultural experience, economic congress, recreation, and the self-justifying "change of place." The habit of automobility, however faddish to disparage, appears thoroughly ingrained in American culture. Even among many of the younger set who have sought to "return to the earth," there is a strong desire to transport themselves regularly to "the action." In our times, the action often unfolds in radii that extend from coast to coast in energy-consumptive links. Endorsing a sedentary and isolated utopia is not the same as living in it.

The fueling of extensive personal transport does not seem amenable to the levels of self-sufficiency to which heating and cooling space may be brought. Grain and wood alcohol compete for the same land and resources as other valued products, food and timber. Although alcohol and food do not compete in a one-to-one ratio, there is still a limit to the land area that can be used for the growing of such biomass. Moreover, the electric car, presently in the process of rapid development and improvement, has not been shown to be either as swift or as versatile as its oil-driven big brother. The need to conserve energy used for personal transport is likely to remain an important element of any strategy for energy sufficiency in the years ahead and is also likely to restrain the urge toward deconcentration.

THE SOLAR CITY

Considerable research has been conducted recently on the fit between solar energy and spatial concentration. The general conclusion is that the city is not as badly formed for the collection of solar energy as might initially have been thought. Peter Pollock describes the situation in terms of four factors: solar access, new cities, retrofit possibilities, and mitigating impacts. Each of these factors is reviewed below.

Solar Access

Pollock explains that solar access involves the protection of a building's roof, face, and surrounding yard from the encroachment of shadowing of the powerful 9:00 A.M. to 3:00 P.M. rays of the sun by neighboring buildings or vegetation. Research by Ralph Knowles and Richard Berry has been conducted on the interaction of "solar envelopes"—the largest volume of a building that will not shade neighboring land parcels—in Los Angeles. The Knowles and Berry study finds that a density of fifty-two dwelling units per acre can be achieved without significant blockage in solar access. Somewhat lesser expectations are held for the densities possible in U.S. cities located farther north than Los Angeles.

New Towns

Milne, Adelson, and Corwin have made studies that examine the land required if a new town were built on the principle of max-imizing the use of solar energy. Using the same amount of land as a typical city of 100,000, the residential sector in the solar new town was found to be capable of achieving self-sufficiency if 80.7 percent of its available roof area were used for collection. The commercial area could collect 67 percent of its needed energy by using about half its parking area and all its rooftop space. The industrial area could collect 18 percent of its needed energy from on-site collectors. However, the researchers found that by expanding the land area in the hypothetical new town by 34.5 percent, all three sectors could achieve energy self-sufficiency.

Solar-energy savings can be combined with conservation of water and fuel for transportation in a properly designed new town, as the plans of architect Sim Van der Ryn demonstrate for his Solar City in Marin County, California. Contrasting Solar City with conventional development, Van der Ryn estimates savings of 80 percent in space and water heating (by solar heating), 26 percent in electricity use (by solar energy) rising to 100 percent with the installation of photovoltaics, 40 percent in transportation (by use of walking and bicycling), 30 percent in food (by on-site production), and 70 percent in water use (by on-site collection and recycling).

Retrofit Possibilities

Pollock notes that Sim Van der Ryn has detailed the viability of water-conserving methods of waste disposal and recycling. Further, Van der Ryn has, with his colleagues in The Farallones Group in San Francisco, also demonstrated methods of energy conservation and self-sufficiency in the already-built environment. The Milne, Adelson, and Corwin study considers the same problem and concludes that an existing city that seeks to meet 25 percent of its energy needs from solar sources would require using 20.2 percent of its residential roof area, 16.4 percent of its total commercial area, and 83.7 percent of its industrial land area for purposes of solar collection. Another study found that the commercial district would need to collect some solar energy from outside its boundaries to meet the 25 percent goal, while the industrial sector would need to rely on other renewable sources than solar energy, such as biomass co-generating systems, in order to provide for 25 percent of its energy needs. This group also pointed to the problems of visual intrusion of solar equipment in high-density areas, as detailed by Jaffee, and the necessity to remove 15 to 30 percent of the tree canopy in low-density residential areas.

Mitigating Factors

Pollock has discussed mitigating factors that also affect land use. They include increased end-use efficiencies of energy, which may lower energy demand (for example, better-insulated hot-water heaters); increased efficiencies in solar technologies; energy supply from outside the city (wind, hydroelectric, ethanol, and methane); non-building sites for collectors (drive-in theaters, parking lots, cemeteries); and changing patterns of land use.

SOLAR LIMITS AND OPPORTUNITIES

The studies upon which Pollock draws share four important points in common. First, their conclusions are highly optimistic regarding the contribution solar energy will be able to make to the urban environment, already built or new. Second, the studies suggest that spatial patterns need not be disrupted by even large infusions of solar hardware. Third, the studies all emerge from research bases in the Western United States and draw on both the urban and physical structure of those locales. And fourth, none of the studies save that by Van der Ryn pays much attention to a factor that consumes nearly 25 percent of our energy—transportation.

Each of these points suggests the limits of an orderly transition to solar energy. The optimism of the solar movement is based on the recognition that a large portion of our needs for heating and cooling could be met by solar sources. Although fewer than one-tenth of 1 percent of the homes in the Western United States, a region of solar abundance, are presently solar heated, it may be a consolation to know that many more of them could be.

The limits of optimism come with the recognition that the sun does not always shine when it is needed to warm our collectors and the wind often stands calm when the windmill's power is needed. Photovoltaic cells will require maintenance and cleaning, and conservation requires a vigilance that will often intrude on visions of the good life. The solar life is not an easy one, however "organic" its vision. It requires a discipline that will be resisted by many Americans for years to come.

The second conclusion, that spatial patterns need not be disrupted by solar hardware, meets its limits in the continuing U.S. preference for nonurban life styles. Solar technology can often be adapted to the urban setting, but there is little doubt that it fits the suburban and rural milieus even more productively. The technology of solar collection, by itself, is rarely an urban inducement. Only when combined with advantages of co-generation or shared walls to conserve heat, or by the desire to reduce transportation costs, does the city demonstrate its solar gains. Even then, the shared wall implies a limit in yard space available for solar collection or vegetable production. There are undeniable limits imposed by decreasing scale in the business of solar collection.

The third conclusion, that solar studies have a Western tilt, may be understandable in terms of the solar potential of the Sunbelt, but the Western studies must certainly be replicated in other climes before their findings can be applied with any confidence. The winter sun shines more weakly in Chicago than in Los Angeles, and its lower declension extends the bulk and height of the solar envelopes of its buildings. Further, the concentration of Chicago's buildings gives rise to potential conflicts among neighbors regarding the aesthetics of solar collectors, as well as their shadows, as Martin Jaffee's research has shown.

Finally, the impact of transportation upon the solar city suggests that, whatever the limits on the other factors, the solar city is a decided possibility. If city dwellers can maintain their present advantage over suburbanites in using less hard energy to heat and cool their homes, even as suburbanites press their modest advantage in converting their homes to solar collection, the city will add greatly to its energy advantage as it moves to the form of the nucleated community. With schools and shopping in walking distance and work within reach of bicycle or bus, the city is not likely to be abandoned in a solar society, however strongly individuals yearn for the half-acre lot.

Will we choose an orderly solar transition? Or will we rather leave the future of our energy patterns in cities and towns to the millions of consumer decisions made within the constraints of the "free-market" system? Is there, in other words, any role for public policy in guiding our energy future?

The Reagan administration has answered the last question with a resounding negative, but the question remains open to debate. Whatever our choice, it would seem prudent that we be alert to the advantages of both concentration and decentralization of population and land use. The dialectic between concentration, with its gains in efficiency, and decentralization, with its benefits of solar generation, can yield the synthesis of their selective combination. This resolution also avoids the dangers inherent in wild swings of policy fluctuation.

If we follow our present hard-path policy, with its suburban and Sunbelt orientation, and then reverse our patterns drastically toward reurbanization when hard-path shortfall rears its likely head, we will have made a great many unwise land use decisions in the interim. If we then wake to the wisdom of selective decentralization as a way of achieving solar stability, we must once more reclaim a great many previously abandoned structures and areas. A better approach may be to recognize the desirability of the multinucleated urban future modeled by diversification, integration, and the concentration of population within emergent centers in present cities, suburbs, and towns — in both Frostbelt and Sunbelt. A future that builds on a past that has anticipated its needs will prove more beneficial than one flowing from a past that sought daily to adapt to rapidly fluctuating energy patterns and perceptions. The development of an energy base of coproduction, delineated in Chapter 7, may be our best assurance of successful adaptation to the vagaries of our energy future.

7

Coproduction: A New Way of Thinking About Energy

Those of us who use energy generally think about it as a necessity that is provided to us by a large corporation; for its use we pay the required price. We are consumers; they are providers. We pay; they supply and usually profit. We grumble about the rising price and occasionally contemplate expressing protest; they explain why costs are rising and supplies are tight.

In perhaps no other arena of our economic society are the lines drawn so starkly between producer and consumer than in the energy area. The energy user seems to have no choice but to accept, pay for, and grumble about the life-sustaining forces that issue from household sockets, gas pipes, oil trucks, and gasoline hoses.

Thus emerge the institutional images of energy politics: greedy oil companies raising prices at the expense of hopeless and impotent consumers; hapless government officials failing to interfere in the workings of energy supply and demand; misguided utility companies turning, of seeming necessity, to nuclear power while their costs skyrocket; community groups becoming more insistent that energy providers should pay more attention to conservation and less to production.

The images leap right out of the hagiology of the American past: the greedy corporate supplier; the ineffectual governmental regulator; the conflictive public-utility executive victimizing the dependent consumer; and the righteously outraged protest organizer. Big versus little, profit versus public good, consumer versus provider— venerable images in the economics of U.S. capitalism.

Apt as this imagery appears to be for understanding many individual and institutional reactions, it does not fully encompass the present reality of energy delivery. Nor does it necessarily serve as a guide to our energy future. Consumers need not remain totally dependent while producers assume all the terrible burdens of provision. In hundreds of U.S. communities, a historic process is underway as consumers and providers discover new roles for themselves as collaborators in the production and conservation of energy. This process may best be seen as one of emerging coproduction, a concept adapted from contemporary political science.

THE CONCEPT OF COPRODUCTION

When political scientists sought to develop explanations of how public services are delivered in cities and towns, the concept of "coproduction" was developed. As Richard Rich, who studied with Elinor Ostrom and her colleagues at the University of Indiana while a series of pioneering studies of service delivery was conducted, writes: "Most public services have the characteristics of being provided through a process in which the *combined* efforts of consumers and service personnel determined the quality and quantity of services actually available."

Thus "public order" in a city is produced not only by the actions of municipal employees—police, courts, and correction officials—but also by their interaction with an alert and watchful citizenry. As Jane Jacobs has noted, the parent watching his or her child at play in the street below and the neighbor seemingly idly chatting on the front steps play important roles in the provision of urban order. Their very presence dissuades the criminal or vandal from striking under their watchful eyes. The vigilance of the urban citizenry performs the tasks of street surveillance with far greater efficiency than the limited ranks of police personnel, who may thereby concentrate their efforts on quick response to reported crime.

As with public order, so with nearly every other municipal service. The cleanliness of streets results from both the proper disposal of trash and its effective collection. The minimization of loss by fire results from citizen attention to prevention and prompt reporting as well as from the skills of the fire department. The provision of adequate shelter involves the attention of home owners and tenants to the maintenance of property as well as the regulatory attention of city-enforcers and licensers. The maintenance of public health results from the prevalence of proper diets and habits adopted by individuals as well as from the availability of doctors, nurses, hospitals, and medicine.

The list of services in which coproduction exists is extended by Rich to include drug abuse, family planning, and nutrition. Programs in each of these areas depend "as much on the efforts of clients to secure and utilize information" as they do upon the abilities of staff members. "Similarly," Rich continues, "one frequently hears that the amount of education a child actually derives from public school attendance is determined at least as much by his or her own effort to learn and parents' support of educational norms as by the efforts of classroom teachers and school administrators."

Rich contends that coproduction is performed in both the "soft" social service areas and the "hard" delivery areas of trash collection and fire prevention. He notes that the benefits of coproduction, like those of public services themselves, "generally represent collective goods for the citizens of the affected areas." That is, if residents "work together to clean a junk-filled, rat-infested vacant lot, everyone in the area enjoys a healthier environment as a result, whether or not" he or she contributed to the cleaning. This gives rise to the problem of the free rider: "Why should I add my contribution to the arduous clean-up task if my neighbors will perform the task anyway, if I conveniently absent myself on the work day?" Rich notes that the citizen must "feel certain that others will contribute enough to make the project a success so that the benefits of volunteering outweigh the costs." Further, governments can "significantly influence this perception by recognizing the potential significance of coproduction, and organizing service delivery procedure so as to take advantage of it."

Coproduction, it is evident, is an important part of the delivery of almost every municipal service. But what of its role in energy, unmentioned by Rich? Is energy the exception? Or is there also a role for the citizen in the provision of energy sufficiency in our cities and towns?

THE COPRODUCTION OF ENERGY

At first glance, energy production does not appear to provide much room for citizen participation. The conventional sources of energy—coal, oil, radioactive minerals—are remote from our communities. The points of energy refinement and generation are usually huge industrial installations protected from citizen intrusion by sophisticated systems of security and defense.

Yet, in hundreds of cities and millions of homes, citizens are playing an organized role in the production and use of energy. In Carbondale, Illinois, for example, energy demand for electricity and fuel oil
declined significantly between 1978 and 1979 through use of a process organized and monitored by a citizens' energy committee. In
Santa Clara County, California, 10,000 motorists have taken the
pledge to join a group called "Energy Fast"; they have reduced their
gasoline use from the national average of sixty gallons per month to
the group's goal of forty gallons per month. In other communities, the
combination of citizen group action and householder awareness has
given far slower rise to the expansion of energy use than forecast by
utilities. This decline in anticipated energy demand has led to revised rate structures and has recast future plans for utility expansion.
Citizen action and householder awareness has encouraged a previously unheard-of willingness on the part of some utility companies to
engage in activities conducive both to energy conservation and the
improved predictability of future demand for their product.

These examples, which are multiplied in the reports of SERI, suggest that the beginnings of energy coproduction are found in the area
of conservation. As both a president of the United States and researchers at the Harvard Business School have noted, conservation is
equivalent to energy production, at least in our present situation.
Former President Carter stated that a barrel of oil saved means that
we need not import that barrel. Stobaugh and Yergin point out: "The
most impelling factor in encouraging conservation action is the cost
of not conserving."

Of course, the time may come when conservation no longer is
equivalent to production. That will be when our energy cushion of
waste has been deflated, and to conserve will mean to deprive one's
self. However, we are far from that situation in a society in which
even our new automobiles yield fewer than twenty-five miles per
gallon, our houses are poorly weatherized, and principles of solar
design have been grossly neglected. The first frontier of coproduction
is indeed conservation and much remains to be accomplished.

To state the matter precisely, energy is coproduced by conservation when individuals reduce their energy use by deliberate plan and
suppliers seek to reestablish demand predictability by establishing
communication with those who purchase their supplies.

Conservation is the first step toward full energy coproduction. This
step is taken by individuals who systematically achieve the
weatherization of their homes—installing adequate insulation,
weather stripping and double glazing their windows and doors,

caulking their door and window frames, installing a flue damper in their heating systems, and wrapping their hot-water heater in insulation. Such actions may cut energy use in a typical home by up to 40 percent, especially when accompanied by energy-conscious temperature settings. Conserving individuals are also likely to reduce their consumption of gasoline for transport to forty gallons a month, or less. Once they have accomplished the full weatherization of their homes, they are ready to benefit from the direct production of energy in their homes.

The installation of a rooftop collector, a solar greenhouse, or a heat-collecting wall signifies entry to the second state of energy coproduction. Now the individual is directly producing energy, and becomes significantly less dependent upon utilities and energy corporations for energy needed for the heating and cooling of space and heating of water. If land surrounding the home is available for additional collection, the on-site energy generated may well suffice for all save extended sunless periods.

A third step toward energy coproduction is taken when groups of neighbors within a community come to the conclusion that it is in their joint interest to explore energy development through a cooperative project. Perhaps their homes lack yard space sufficient for the installation of a storage unit for the heat generated by their rooftop collectors. Or perhaps the pattern of shading between one neighbor's trees and another's house makes the sharing of available solar potential desirable. In such cases, joint projects of energy development might emerge, perhaps accompanied by other neighborhood projects designed to reduce energy use, such as cooperative vegetable gardens or ride-sharing programs.

Fourth on the path to full energy coproduction might be the development of a neighborhood system of energy co-generation, perhaps taking advantage of cooperation with a nearby industrial or institutional power plant. In such a case, the waste heat loosed by the power plant might be transferred, perhaps by the piping of water, to provide heat and hot water to all the homes in the area of the plant, thus providing the economics of reuse implied by co-generation.

Finally, one can imagine a situation in which a landowner or a group of neighbors develop such productive capacity from their solar installations that they are able to generate significantly more energy than they require for the heating and cooling of their homes. Much of this excess could be used for the propulsion of their electric automobiles, but some will remain for sale to the area's power grid. At this stage individuals will have become primary producers of energy, and the public utilities will be playing the facilitative role of buying and distributing the excess power.

These images of coproduction, especially the last several stages, will seem fanciful to many. But legislation already embodied in the Public Utilities Regulatory Policies Act, passed in 1978, requires electric grids to purchase energy generated cooperatively. Such buybacks are presently in operation in many locations. By the year 2000, some 20 million individual power stations are foreseen by community energy specialist David Morris.

The magnitude of the reorientation in the relationship between coproducing home owner and utility company is well illustrated by the case of John LaMar, a physician in Pennsville, New Jersey. Dr. LaMar installed a windmill in his backyard in August 1980 and immediately achieved a savings of more than one-half of his electric bill. So far, so good. As LaMar put it, "The beauty of this thing is that all I have to do is just plug it into an outlet in my house." The price of the mill was $6,500. First month's energy savings came to over $100.

Then LaMar approached the Atlantic Electric Company regarding their interest in buying back the surplus electricity produced by the windmill. As he explains it, "When I am producing more electricity than I can use, it flows back into their system. It's completely compatible."

The utility company indicated it would buy his electricity, but only at the wholesale rate of 2.5 cents per kilowatt hour. When his windmill is not providing all the electricity he needs, LaMar buys power from the utility company at the rate of 8 cents per kilowatt hour. A utility spokesman explained the policy: "He is selling it wholesale and we are selling it at retail. I have no argument whatsoever with that statement. Why should we pay more?" He explained that while the cost of buying from LaMar was of little consequence, the amount would have to be spread out among the 320,000 customers of the utility. Such a burden might become significant as the number of backyard windmills increased, the official added.

At this writing, state officials are seeking to develop a pricing policy that would provide a clear set of regulations and rate structures. These deliberations are welcomed by both the coproducers and the public utilities. As the vice-president of a major utility company put it: The new means of energy production "are the coming thing, and we are anticipating the fact that more people are going to cogenerate, set up windmills and conserve electricity and that it might impact on our operating costs."

Karl Hess draws on his experience in organizing "community technology" projects in both urban and rural areas:

> For many communities these days the first and most obvious place to start any community technology demonstration or experimentation is in the area of energy. . . . Experiments and demonstrations in alternative sources of energy are a quick entryway to the interests of most communities. The most obviously intriguing part of it is solar energy. Fortunately, it is the part most susceptible to community technology demonstration, even in northern climes.

Hess suggests that a community begin with a project aimed at providing solar-heated hot water. A number of homes and a few smaller public buildings should be chosen to demonstrate the feasibility of the technology. The community might move on to projects that store solar heat. He notes that abandoned quarries might serve for either heat storage or, sequentially, "cold storage" for air conditioning use. Hess adds, in regard to solar energy:

> The community technology group has another responsibility and opportunity. It should keep very close tabs on the development both of chemical and mechanical energy storage systems and also on the development of devices for direct conversion of solar energy to electrical energy. The speed with which photovoltaic cells for direct conversion are dropping in cost makes me strongly suspect that we are on the edge of an energy revolution more far-reaching than any we have ever known. Should that revolution have a moving effect only at the most centralized and remote levels of social authority, we may be in for real trouble if an energy source that could be dramatically liberating is instead bureaucratically or economically shackled to the purposes of either big business or big government.
>
> Community technology groups working at the local level would do well to keep their friends, their town officials, and their inner-city groups closely advised on the possibilities of using photovoltaic energy *before* it becomes chained to one or another corporate interest, either government or private.

Bruce Stokes cautions that this process of consumer development will be neither quick nor easy:

> The transition to an era of greater dependence on renewable energy resources will take time. Consumers experience the vulnerability of dependence on nonrenewable energy resources only indirectly,

through price rises and periodic shortages. But the initial capital costs and maintenance problems of solar technologies affect people directly and may dull their enthusiasm, despite the long-term advantages of solar power. Moreover, some solar applications are novel, and people are suspicious of new technologies until they have mastered them. The important thing for consumers is that solar technology is something they *can* master.

Rather than being a fanciful dream, then, it would appear that coproduction may become a widespread reality in the decades ahead. Beginning as conservation, the concept extends to include direct energy production on a household and community level. The societal implications of such developments might be expected to be substantial.

IMPLICATIONS OF COPRODUCTION: COOPERATION OR PRIVATISM?

The social implications of coproduction have excited the greatest attention in the energy literature. The coming of an age of decentralized solar collection has been viewed as highly conducive to the emergence of highly sociable and cooperative life ways. Karl Hess presents the vision rhapsodically:

> My own interest is the responsibility of people to *be* responsible for their own lives and, with their neighbors, for their public space and actions. To sing their own songs. To make their own inventions. To be onstage and out of the audience. To love and not just yearn.
>
> To build and not just envy. To light that candle which is so much better than cursing the darkness. To be as much as the human condition can sustain, rather than being only what a system can allow. To be. To do. That is community technology.

One may well question this assumption regarding the fit between coproduction and social change. Americans might pursue solar generation in the same spirit of individualism with which they buy gasoline for their cars or oil for their home burners. Who has, gets. Why should the generation of solar power be any different?

Believers in "solar life ways" respond that the spirit of the frontier will be reborn in a solar age. People will spend more time outside of their houses in the visible pursuit of energy collection—installing their collectors and cultivating their vegetable patches. These activities will naturally give rise, they argue, to an increase in neighborly conversa-

tion and the development of new feelings of warmth and collaboration.

On the other hand, solar innovations might simply come to be seen
as just another way to heat a house. Individual home owners might
contract separately for their installations. Neighborly interaction in-
spired by such solar conversion might be limited to a modest amount
of kibitzing over the fence.

Images of a solar society in which justice, cooperation, and mutual
care flourish may be too quickly drawn. These values will not sprout
full-blown from any technology. They will need to be articulated and
nurtured by a process of dialogue and decision.

It is when energy begins to be coproduced on a cooperative scale
that the first substantial steps toward the value transformation of a
solar society might be expected. When citizens begin to require
cooperation and support from each other in meeting their energy
needs, their images of society may shift. As they take charge of collectively reorienting their resource use to sustain human growth, rather
than viewing themselves as dependent consumers of energy provided by corporations, new images of community self-reliance may
emerge.

To the active producer, every energy-related choice is too important to be left to remote captains of industry or overseas oil ministries.
Coproducers will want a say in their energy decisions. The time and
personal energy they will have to devote to these questions will, of
course, be limited. Citizen participation in energy production will
face many of the same constraints that have faced citizen participation in antipoverty policy, housing, criminal justice, and environmental affairs. Restrictive factors will include the different degrees of participation by persons of higher and lower social class, the "mobilization of bias" against citizen participation, and the potential for
stalemate as an outcome of participation.

All three factors will surely plague the coproduction of energy. Persons of higher income will find themselves with greater opportunities
to develop financially attractive coproduction situations than those
preoccupied with assembling sufficient funds to pay for the next rent
bill or grocery trip. Established economic and governmental officials
will seek to restrict citizen interest in energy policy to those issues the
officials view as legitimate. Many will say that appropriate issues most
certainly do not include influencing utility company decisions on the
installation of nuclear power or automobile company decisions on
the production of electric cars. The third factor will also be evident:
Some citizens will seek to restrain those of their neighbors who seek

to erect windmills, orient their windows to the south, or protect their backyard collectors from the growth of towering oaks on adjoining property.

But coproduction differs in several significant ways from previous forms of citizen participation. Unlike those experiences of participation in public policy issues in which citizens were provided solely with roles of potential influence over policy decisions, energy coproduction provides centrally for producer roles. The citizen who seeks only to fight city hall (or the local power and light company) will win or lose on the specific issue joined. But the energy coproducer will have directly reduced energy expenditures by introducing a new form of conservation or by installing a solar collector.

The linkage between self-interest and concern for the public good distinguishes citizen participation in energy coproduction from previous forms of citizen participation. That linkage suggests that energy coproduction will prove to be a far more significant force for societal change than were its predecessors. In typical forms of citizen participation, the individual is assessed heavy costs in time and energy and has no guarantee that a comparable return will emerge from that participation. The citizen participant often struggles for the achievement of a policy that benefits a large class of individuals, but he or she may gain only a little from a victory. The energy coproducer may similarly participate in policy questions, but his or her participation rests on a firm base of self-interest in energy-cost reduction. This base should do much to assure the firmness and durability of the coproduction movement.

Why are individuals likely to join together on behalf of energy conservation and change? First, the costs in both time and effort of developing skills and knowledge of energy coproduction will be significant. If individuals can pool these skills and knowledge, all stand to save from the gains of collaboration. Second, energy coproduction will surely demonstrate economies in scale, just as does the production of most other economic goods. A single charging block for all electric cars in a neighborhood, jointly owned by the neighborhood electric cooperative, may prove more economical than the installation of a similar facility in every private garage. The cooperative itself may well prove a more efficacious means to produce solar energy than a series of individual installations. Cooperation may promote the development of management and maintenance skills in some participants and thereby relieve the burdens each home owner might otherwise carry. Finally, the gains in sociability and common enterprise might themselves prove sufficiently rewarding to inspire at least some individuals to seek to develop and maintain such a cooperative organization.

Ultimately, the establishment of thousands of neighborhood solar coproduction cooperatives nationally would create a substantial organizational and political force. The energy coproduction movement would surely give rise to regional and national coalitions that would advocate a variety of positions on issues such as nuclear power, soft-path energy development, and energy conservation. From the interaction of solar practitioners in these cooperative organizations would emerge, as well, an ongoing forum for the development of new and ingenious methods to advance decentralized energy production and energy conservation.

CRITERIA FOR COPRODUCTION

The innumerable ways in which energy can and will be coproduced in the years ahead may perhaps be anticipated by criteria for coproduction to define the boundaries of the phenomenon and indicate the territory that it may one day cover. The criteria should prove useful to those who seek to devise new and better ways to use available energy more wisely. Seven criteria for energy coproduction are:

1. Use energy resources to the fullest extent.
2. Choose methods with relatively low capital costs first.
3. Introduce methods that quickly show results.
4. Disrupt established patterns of social life to a minimal degree.
5. Coproduction should be phased in as part of a national strategy or movement.
6. Recognize and exploit the hidden and unanticipated benefits of coproduction.
7. Use electronic communications to facilitate conservation activities.

Each of these criteria will now be discussed and developed.

Criterion 1

Use energy resources to the fullest extent. Jeremy Rifkin has noted that we moderns do not really consume products, but rather use them briefly and then discard them. Such is certainly the case with energy we employ. It often receives the briefest employment and then disappears in the form of waste heat before anything approaching its full use can be realized.

The essence of conservation involves the more efficacious use of available resources, the minimization of their waste, and their joint use or reuse to the maximum degree feasible. Thus, the energy coproducer strives first to use as little energy as possible and to cooperatively use or reuse energy to the maximum degree. Conservation, co-generation, reuse, and shared use are basic elements of energy coproduction.

Criterion 2

First choose methods that involve relatively low capital costs. Coproduction may require new capital in the construction of solar collectors or piping for the transmission of co-generated heat. These costs, while they may be substantial for a given project, must be seen as reasonable in terms of the pay-back of the coproduction project. That is, the costs should not saddle future generations with the obligation to pay for energy consumed by those who have gone before, as so many of our current nuclear installations do. Energy gains should be enjoyed by all those who invest in coproduction, and the life of these projects should extend beyond the period required to finance their investment.

The second criterion reminds us that capital itself will be limited in the years ahead; that will make the simplest forms of coproduction even more attractive. The building of all new homes and buildings in accord with principles of passive solar design, the shared use of as much energy for transportation as possible, and the fullest use of unprocessed food are all consistent with the principle of "minimum feasible capital" for the co-generation of energy.

Criterion 3

Introduce methods that quickly show results. A relatively short time-horizon of successes will hasten the introduction of coproduction. Among the greatest benefits to society of the widespread distribution of coproduction is protection against the social and economic disaster that threatens us in the form of hard-energy disruption. We need energy coproduction, and we need it now. The physical and social technology of coproduction will surely be advanced in the years ahead. The capacity it gives us to withstand the most crippling blows of energy shortfall makes it a primary element in any national strategy of energy independence.

Insisting on a relatively short time-line for energy coproduction will further encourage the development of conservation and enhance capital-minimizing forms of energy development. Future generations may have the leisure to introduce coproduction schemes that take decades to develop and introduce. Our needs are more immediate. We now know enough about solar energy, co-generation, and conservation to be able to focus on the immediate gains that are available to us. The short-term successes will do much, in turn, to stimulate long-term developments.

Criterion 4

Disrupt, to a minimal degree, established patterns of social life. The introduction of coproduction may ultimately be revolutionary in its impact. The initial phases will proceed far more efficaciously if they are implemented in a spirit of incrementalism, individual and neighboring initiative, and conserving prudence.

Americans are a skeptical lot and have grown highly resistant to the siren calls of social revolution in these past decades of grand visions and limited advance. While a small minority of temporarily hip and young new solar pioneers may sustain a vision of social revolution by coproduction, the action of the vast majority of more conventional Americans will determine our energy future. These prudent persons will be persuaded by the economic benefits of coproduction and its insurance against the ravages of sudden shortfall. They will not welcome innovations that drastically disrupt their ways of life. Instead, they prudently will turn to coproduction when it is shown to be necessary and profitable. The case should be made to them with the same probity and concern with which life insurance is marketed. Just as the first life insurance companies were community cooperatives, so will be the first successful ventures in energy coproduction.

Criterion 5

Coproduction should be phased in as a part of a consistent national strategy or movement. It is to be hoped that energy planners in governmental and corporate life will recognize the superiority of coproduction strategies over the desperate gambles involved in hard-path escalation. However likely it is that these elites will cling to their faith in the nuclear fix or the fusion gamble, an energy policy based on an orderly transition to renewable energy and low entropy will likely be part of any energy future. Failing its acceptance by policy makers, the strategy of coproduction will nonetheless be advanced by legislative facilitation, judicial protection, community organization, and consumer choice. The need to defend against a potentially hostile set of governmental and corporate decision makers will itself be a powerful incentive for advocates and practitioners of coproduction to join in community and national organizations with genuine political clout.

Criterion 6

Recognize and exploit the hidden and unanticipated benefits of energy coproduction wherever possible. An energy-conserving idea may be so obvious as to avoid discovery, whether it be in a home, a city, or a nation. The search to develop the art and science of energy coproduction should receive great attention, and there are certainly many serendipitous discoveries to be made along the way.

Criterion 7

Use electronic communications to facilitate energy conservation through coproduction activities. As we increasingly enter the "wired society," energy coproduction may be facilitated in many ways by systems of rapid communication. Not only will such systems replace the need for much personal transit, but they will speed the development of new forms of energy coproduction by linking consumer groups nationally and internationally in a myriad of interacting networks.

How likely is it that such a vision of energy coproduction might become firmly established in the lives of Americans? The following chapter explores the readiness Americans express toward the elements of coproduction, as reflected in a range of studies of public opinion and social change.

8

The Emerging Solar Majority

The vision of energy coproduction is based on a set of principles long established and deeply embedded in American life. Among these principles are those of self-help, voluntary action, and economic self-interest.

Americans have never trusted their personal destinies to social institutions—whether governmental or corporate—but have preferred to grapple with and resolve their own problems when possible. Thus, early traditions of cooperative house building and community resource development continue to the present in the forms of many millions of formal and informal groups who work with each other to resolve their own concerns. These groups, ranging from neighborhood child-care arrangements to anti-alcoholism support, are a formidable aspect of the tradition of community self-help and self-reliance in the United States.

Our structures of voluntary action grow out of that tradition of self-help and cooperative problem solving. Many of these arrangements have become embodied in formal organizations that are aimed at the broad alleviation of distress or the common advocacy of policy change. Ranging from the services provided by the American Red Cross or the Literacy Volunteers of America, on the service side, to the changes demanded as needed by a suburban civic association or an inner-city minority neighborhood association, the voluntary sector hosts more than 6 million groups and organizations seeking to better conditions of life for themselves and those who are identified to be in special risk or need. These groups, few of which provide any tangible financial rewards for their members, are seen by social scientists as innovators of programs and conservers of established societal truths.

The third base upon which energy coproduction rests is that of economic self-interest. Firmly established as the "economic freedom" upon which so much of the American experience has developed, the ultimate principle here is that the individual knows best his or her own wants and needs and that the marketplace provides an effective locus for the meeting of those needs. This principle is, however, often challenged by critics from the left and right: the leftists note that those with money are far more powerful in the market than those without; many rightists violate the principle by manipulating the market forces through advertising and state protection of failing enterprises. Nonetheless, the principle of economic self-interest remains firmly established in rhetoric.

The purpose of this chapter is to assess the readiness of Americans, in the 1980s and beyond, to commit themselves to the various activities entailed in energy coproduction—from altering their patterns of commuting and residence to engaging in conservation, from moving toward the direct production of energy in their homes to joining with neighbors in community energy development. The data upon which the arguments of this chapter will be based are drawn from surveys on aspects of coproduction in recent years.

VIEWS ON ENERGY CONSERVATION IN THE UNITED STATES

In 1978, Marvin Olsen admirably summarized American views on energy conservation: "Americans are slowly awakening to the realization that the energy problem is indeed real and permanent, and that the simplest and most effective means of averting a catastrophic energy crisis within the next 20 to 30 years is to begin reducing our energy consumption now. . . . Without doubt . . . energy conservation will become an increasingly dominant theme in American society during the next few years."

Olsen cited findings regarding the degree to which the public had accepted energy conservation and its practice. These findings were:

1. Most people understand the essence of the energy problem.
2. Belief in the reality of the energy crisis is fairly widespread.
3. Most people have taken a few minimal conservation actions.
4. Relatively few people have taken major conservation actions.
5. Socioeconomic status is a major determinant of conservation actions.
6. Education and occupation, two other major components of socioeconomic status, are also directly related to acceptance of energy conservation, though not as strongly as income.

7. Age is the only sociodemographic characteristic that is clearly related to conservation actions.
8. Acceptance of proposed conservation measures is fairly widespread.

If we review these eight propositions individually and add to their consideration some data collected since Olsen wrote, we may be in a position not only to test his hypotheses but also to see if we can determine the direction and speed in which American opinion may be changing on these questions.

1. Most people understand the essence of the energy problem. Olsen concluded that most people understand what an energy crisis involves. His conclusion was based on the response, in 1976, to the question, "What is your understanding of what the energy problem is all about?" He found that 58 percent of the polled population gave quite satisfactory responses. ("Demand is greater than supply." "Natural resources are being used up." "Energy is being used wastefully." or "U.S. dependence on foreign oil supply.") Another 23 percent of the sample gave "relevant but less precise responses" involving the need to conserve energy or its high costs.

The fact that four out of five Americans can define an energy crisis seems encouraging; however, more recent data suggest that many Americans are not aware of important factual evidence that might indicate the presence of such a crisis. In 1978, when the United States was importing 46 percent of its oil from foreign sources, only 57 percent of a national polled sample believed that we were importing 35 percent or more. By the following year, when the import of oil reached 47 percent, the proportion who believed that we were still dependent on foreign sources for one-third or more of our oil had dropped to 43 percent. Even more startling is the Gallup finding that in mid-1979 only 46 percent of a sample reported that we needed to import "some oil" from other countries. A large proportion of Americans, it appears, finds it difficult to acknowledge the fact that oil is imported, much less our national dependence upon those supplies.

When these findings are put together, can Olsen's claim that Americans understand "the essence" of the energy problem be sustained? Or, rather, does it seem that while most Americans can define an energy crisis, nearly half of them find themselves unable to comprehend one of the most prominent elements of an energy crisis, the dependence upon imported oil? Modification of Olsen's statement does seem in order, perhaps along the lines of the statement: "While most people can define an energy crisis, half the population is unaware of the basic facts of our national energy dependence upon foreign oil."

2. *Belief in the energy crisis is fairly widespread.* Olsen cites a number of studies reported in 1976 and 1977 that indicated "approximately half the U.S. population believes that this country faces a serious long-term energy problem." Further, of the half that believe in the energy crisis, "roughly half view the energy situation as an immediate and permanent problem, while the other half do not consider it to be a problem now but expect it to become a serious crisis by the end of the century."

More recent data indicate that a rather steady 80 percent of the population view the energy crisis as either "very serious" or "fairly serious" when the third choice is "not at all serious." Thus, in August 1979, 47 percent of those responding to a poll viewed the energy crisis as very serious, while 35 percent responded that it was fairly serious.

Other data may be read to indicate less willingness to view the energy problem as real. For example, when asked to choose between viewing energy shortages as real or as contrived by oil companies, most Americans chose to see the shortages as contrived. Or when asked if they agreed with President Carter that we are running out of oil, only one-fourth of those polled reported that things were "as bad as that" in mid-1979. Such questions appear to be tapping two themes simultaneously: the incredulity with which Americans approach their political and economic institutions and the seriousness with which they view the energy situation. A better indicator of their perceptions on the seriousness of the energy problems is provided by asking the question directly. And responses to that question show a steady 80 percent identifying the energy problem as serious since 1977, with no signs of decline in the strength of that opinion.

As for longer-term perceptions of the seriousness of the energy crisis, a national survey in 1977 showed that 60 percent of the population polled thought the energy crisis would be "very serious" in ten years, and 69 percent of a Michigan sample reported that the energy crisis would be serious in the "distant future."

Thus, it would appear that the ranks are steadily growing of those who find the energy problem to be portentous, both in the present and the future. At the same time, however, a sense of confidence appears to be developing that asserts our national ability to resolve the energy problem. As Richman summarizes it:

Public concern about world oil scarcity and U.S. dependence on foreign oil has lessened, even as concern about short-term energy shortages has increased. Roper found that the proportion who believed "the world's supply of oil" would last 100 years or more nearly doubled between early 1977 and early 1979 (from 22 to 40 percent), while the proportion who expected the world's oil supply to be depleted within 25 years fell from 24 percent to 15 percent.

Americans remain inveterate optimists about energy. Fully half of a national sample polled in mid-1979 agreed that we could "get along without importing foreign oil" over the next five years, the same proportion that made the claim in 1975. Only 7 percent claimed to be "not optimistic at all" about our long-term ability to resolve our energy problems, when asked in 1979; 43 percent reported that they were "very optimistic," and another 43 percent agreed that they were somewhat optimistic.

These data suggest that Olsen's statement might be revised to read, "While belief in the seriousness of the energy crisis is widespread, Americans remain highly confident that it will ultimately be resolved."

3. Most people have taken a few minimal conservation actions. To support this conclusion, Olsen cited a number of studies that showed between half and three-fourths of the population were conserving energy by reducing heating and lighting or by driving less. In general, these were actions that required "minimal effort and expense and did not significantly alter people's usual life styles."

A Gallup survey in early 1979 presented a list of twelve conservation behaviors. Of the sample polled, 83 percent were at that time engaged in some of the listed behaviors — 44 percent had turned down their thermostats, 33 percent had curtailed their driving (51 percent by September, after the return of gas lines), 27 percent were turning off lights more frequently than before, 15 percent were generally conserving electricity, 12 percent had insulated their homes, 10 percent had cut down on use of appliances, and so on to the 2 percent who were using less hot water. The average respondent who reported conserving energy claimed two means by which this end was being accomplished.

Other research confirms the acceptability of these simple conservation efforts. For example, nearly half of a sample polled in Washington state reported that it was easy to accept heating limits of 65°, and nearly two-thirds of the same sample found air conditioning limits of 85° similarly acceptable. One may, of course, wonder if residents in a less temperate climate would be so tolerant.

Overall, however, Americans ranked conservation second on a list of possible choices for primary reliance to assure energy adequacy by the year 2000 (35 percent ranked it first, while only 3 percent ranked it last).

Olsen concluded his discussion about these "minimal conservation actions" by noting that "these practices produce only minimal energy savings." This conclusion appears to require substantial modification in light of the recent leveling in oil and electricity consumption and the success the United States has had in reducing the flow of imported oil. Such behaviors as the alteration of driving patterns and the purchase of gasoline-efficient automobiles are beginning to make dramatic inroads into historic patterns of growth in energy consumption. His generalization might now better read: "Almost everyone has taken a number of conservation actions, and as a partial result, historic patterns of energy growth have been stabilized."

4. *Relatively few people have taken major conservation actions.* In supporting this generalization, Olsen notes that fewer than 20 percent of the population polled reported engaging in any costly or significant activity of conservation. A comparison of recent findings with those he cited indicates:

- Fewer people car pooling in 1979 (3 percent) than in 1976 (10 percent).
- No change in the number of people riding public transportation to and from work (8 percent in 1979 and 1976).
- Twelve percent insulated their homes in 1979, as against 9 percent in 1975.
- Fewer than 20 percent of the working population continues to get to work by means other than private, single-passenger-driven automobile in 1979, continuing the practice that prevailed in 1974.

More recently, a national sample of home owners was asked about intentions regarding solar installation. Twenty-eight percent had given the matter some attention: 1 percent of all home owners had already installed a solar system, 3 percent definitely planned to, 16 percent may install a solar system, and 8 percent had decided against a system. Individuals who had made positive decisions had higher incomes, were younger, and particularly, were likely to have received more education than the others. Regionally, there was considerable variation—the Pacific and Mountain states had the highest percentage (29) of solar enthusiasts and the Southern states the lowest (11).

These data give no indication, then, that Olsen's generalization should be changed: "Relatively few people have taken major conservation steps, and the pace of this activity is not dramatically increasing."

5. *Socioeconomic status is a major determinant of conservation actions.* In explaining the impact of status on conservation, Olsen writes that "as a general principle, the higher one's socioeconomic status, the more likely one is to adopt energy-conserving practices and to support energy conservation policies." This principle holds, Olsen contends, because higher-income persons use much of their energy for "nonvital or luxury" purposes and thereby have more latitude than do low-income persons for reducing consumption without changing life styles. Higher-income persons remain heavier energy users than low-income persons even after they have effected their conservation savings. This conclusion appears to stand unchanged: "Socioeconomic status is a major determinant of conservation actions."

6 and 7. *Education, occupation, and age are also related to energy conservation behavior.* Olsen's conclusions regarding the impact of education and occupation (directly related to conservation, though not as strongly as income) and age are also unchanged. Regarding age, Olsen finds that "younger people are generally more conserving of energy and older people less conserving, although middle-aged people tend to be particularly concerned about reducing home heating costs, while older people are especially likely to cut back on driving." Differences in conservation behavior by sex and race appear unclear, and the latter is probably largely determined by socioeconomic status. Once again, there do not appear to be any more recent data to challenge the adequacy of these conclusions to contemporary society: "Education, occupation, and age are closely related to conservation actions."

8. *Acceptance of proposed conservation measures is fairly widespread.* Olsen notes that "surprisingly large numbers" of people indicate acceptance of a wide variety of rather stringent energy conservation policies, although acceptance of the least disruptive proposals appears to be higher. Nevertheless, temperature and lighting controls in public buildings were accepted by 88 percent in a 1974 polled sample; energy conservation standards for new buildings, cars, and appliances were accepted by 85 percent in a 1976 study; and mandatory lowering of electricity consumption was accepted by 80 percent in two 1976 studies.

By 1977 other policy changes became approved by over 60 percent in a number of polled samples. Over 80 percent approved tax rebates for insulation and solar installation; over 70 percent favored requiring utilities to lower off-peak rates; over 80 percent favored strict enforcement of the 55-mile-per-hour speed limit; over 70 percent favored requiring appliances to be energy efficient, even if at a higher cost to the buyer; and over 70 percent favored allowing insulation provided by utility companies to be tax-deductible. Energy conservation is viewed as a field open to the expansion of public policy. The expansion of appropriate governmental regulation and tax revision in this area is widely supported by the general public. Olsen's generalization might now be put with even more vigor: "Acceptance of proposed conservation measures is widespread indeed."

We may now restate Olsen's propositions, as updated:

1. While most people can define an energy crisis, half the population is unaware of the basic facts of our dependence upon foreign oil.
2. While belief in the seriousness of the energy crisis is widespread, Americans remain highly confident that it will utlimately be resolved.
3. Almost everyone has taken a number of conservation actions, and as a partial result, historic patterns of energy growth have been stabilized.
4. Relatively few people have taken major conservation steps, and the pace of this activity is not dramatically increasing.
5. Socioeconomic status is a major determinant of conservation actions.
6,7. Education, occupation, and age are also closely related to conservation actions.
8. Acceptance of proposed conservation measures is widespread indeed.

Reviewing our modifications of Olsen's propositions, we find an overall pattern of continuing acceptance of conservation, but certainly no radical discontinuity between the 1977-and-before world he sought to describe and the 1981-and-before world updated here. Perhaps the shape of things to come can be further clarified through some questions no pollster has yet thought to ask.

What, for instance, can be said about support by Americans for the three alternative major energy ideologies outlined in Chapter 1 — energy plenitude, pragmatism, and transformation? What can be said about the expectations of Americans regarding the magnitude and shape of any energy transformations that may be coming? How do Americans divide regarding their present patterns of conservation behavior? How do they view the future conservation behaviors that may be necessary? What impact will any and all of these changes have for their life styles in the years ahead? How will these changes contribute to or detract from the satisfactions Americans anticipate?

A RESEARCH AGENDA FOR ENERGY LIFE STYLES

Belief, behavior, and life style should be central topics on the social science research agenda on energy futures: belief—because we start with the understandings of the moment and build from that base to try to understand the future; behavior—because our actions are themselves embedded in patterns we inherit from the past, and these actions are the starting point from which our future acts will develop; and life style—because the ways we live gratify or frustrate us in proportion to our expectations, and our images of the future will determine, at least in part, how we will experience that future.

Ideally, research findings would be available to inform us of energy beliefs, behaviors, and anticipated life styles so that we might be able to chart likely future social responses to different energy configurations. In reality, however, research has focused on a relatively narrow range of questions of belief and behavior and has almost entirely avoided probing anticipated life styles. We need a broader research agenda for the study of energy futures, one that draws on the various social and applied behavioral sciences. Three possible foci for such an agenda are presented below.

1. How are energy ideologies distributed? Evidence suggests that the three ideological camps of plenitude, pragmatism, and transformation are of about equal strength. A method of defining these ideologies should be developed; a continuing monitoring of changes in relative strength would be highly useful.

Data indicate that approximately one-third of the population takes the position that our hard-energy reliance is both ill-advised and undependable. Roper has routinely asked respondents to place themselves in one of four camps in interpreting oil shortages, for instance, and one of those positions claims that "there is a very real shortage and the problem will get worse during the next 5 to 10 years." The other three positions see the oil shortages as short-run or contrived. Between 1974 and 1979, anywhere from 21 to 40 percent took the position that the oil shortage was both real and long-term. The mean agreeing with the position was 29 percent.

Questions on nuclear energy also indicate substantial disenchantment with its merits. Gallup found in 1979 that 39 percent disapproved of nuclear energy as a replacement for oil. A Resources for the Future survey found that 38 percent thought that nuclear energy was "dangerous" or "not as safe as solar energy." On the other hand, less than one-third of the same sample (20 percent) agreed that existing nuclear plants should be shut down. However, two-thirds of that sample favored no further building of nuclear plants. (A diametrically opposite ratio, two to one in favor of additional nuclear construction, prevailed in 1977, in the days before the Three Mile Island accident.)

It would appear that the greatest proportion of these hard-path disbelievers are in actuality soft-path optimists. The Harris poll in 1979 found that only 7 percent of the population holds a pessimistic view about the nation's ability to resolve its energy difficulties. Those who find the hard path ill-advised or in the process of exhaustion are apparently convinced that the soft path offers a satisfactory resolution to our difficulties.

As for hard-path optimism, 29 percent of a 1976 sample expressed willingness to accept the health risks of nuclear development rather than to restrict the use of nuclear energy. By 1979, the number viewing nuclear energy as "very safe" had dropped to 15 percent, according to the Resources for the Future poll. Further, only 23 percent of that survey favored continuing to build nuclear plants. However, 44 percent of the respondents to a 1979 Gallup survey expressed approval of nuclear energy as a replacement for oil, a useful reminder that surveyed opinions vary in their solidity and depth.

Hard-path optimists have rallied to the belief that oil is not disappearing precipitously. A rather steady 45 percent respond to the Roper options on oil shortages with the contention that the oil shortages of the 1970s were all contrived, and another 20 percent find the shortages that did exist were only short-term. In response to a 1979 Roper question, four in seven persons with an opinion on the length of time world oil supplies are likely to last indicated 100 years or more. Thus, the best estimate of the size of the hard-path-optimist category would fall between 25 percent and 50 percent.

Between the optimists for the soft and hard paths stand the pragmatists and those who are undecided who form between 25 percent and 40 percent of the respondents to most questions. Responses to the Roper questions suggest that opinion may be aggregating at the two polar positions of hard path and soft path support rather than in the middle. In any case, the situation appears quite fluid, responding dramatically to such events as Three Mile Island or the return of gasoline lines. Will the replacement of a pragmatic liberal by a hard-energy optimist as president of the United States make any substantial difference in prevailing opinion? Or will opinion remain most strongly influenced by dramatic energy events?

2. Are Americans likely to engage in strenuous energy conservation? Data reviewed earlier in this chapter suggest that most Americans are engaging in one or two forms of modest energy conservation. Yet few of us have committed ourselves to a thoroughgoing and comprehensive pattern of energy conservation. Data on anticipated energy conservation show that majorities favor a variety of rather stringent energy-conservation policies. A large number of individuals contemplate participating in such energy conservation without serious difficulty.

The sample polled in Washington state by Dillman and her associates found nearly half accepting heat limits of 65° "easily" and nearly two-thirds accepting summer air-conditioning limits of 85°. Limits on occupied space for winter heating were also seen as acceptable by this sample. Other studies have found people willing to shift modes of personal transport in order to accommodate changing energy patterns.

Responding to a pollster's questions about energy conservation clearly is different from implementing that conservation behavior on a regular and systematic basis. The apparent willingness of Americans to accept stringent conservation behaviors and policies is countered by the realities of slippage that occur in real-life processes of conservation. Thus, Darley and his associates discovered in detailed research on a community conservation experience in New Jersey that energy waste is not confined to a small group of "energy hogs. In fact, our Twin Rivers study and others suggest that most of us are high consumers of certain kinds of energy for certain kinds of use, and low consumers in other situations. In Twin Rivers, for instance, people who used a great deal of natural gas during the winter for heat were not always the ones who used the most during the summer for air conditioning."

Darley and his associates conclude that energy conservation depends upon working successfully with a wide range of individual attitudes and behavior. They suggest the creation of an Energy Conservation Corps in which "trained people would be available to diagnose the energy-conservation potential of houses, to help energy-conservation pioneers carry out those tasks that they can do themselves, to provide them with the expertise necessary to specify exactly how contractors should build, and to carry word of the results to other homeowners."

Our most certain knowledge about how we shall conserve energy under duress will surely come from experimental studies of actual shortfall experiences or the detailed monitoring of reactions to experiential simulations of such situations. The research of psychologists Stanley Milgram and Philip Zimbardo has shown the unpredictable nature of responses to crisis. Energy research could seek to identify dimensions of future behavior that might emerge under the duress that will surely accompany sudden and prolonged energy shortfall.

3. What of future life styles and satisfaction? We have almost no data as to how people view themselves living in the future and the personal satisfaction or dissatisfaction they anticipate from such futures. The sociology of the future is a topic that should increasingly engage social researchers, however, it will probably be from futures simulations that our most reliable data will emerge.

While survey data are not complete when it comes to personal adaptations to energy futures, several themes may be discerned. First, Americans do not want to return to the city. They are wary of cluster design, even though such architecture is increasingly predominating in the new construction of townhouses and condominiums. Second, Americans in substantial numbers are exploring the potential of solar energy. They appear ready to take increasing advantage of its use in the years ahead. Third, Americans seem willing to undertake stringent steps toward personal energy conservation, including mandatory insulation, temperature limits, and reduction of living space in hard-to-heat rooms. Their new-found taste for energy-efficient automobiles has already led to decreases in gasoline consumption. Americans appear to be hunkering in to their present homes and communities with the hope that they will not be required to uproot themselves, particularly to an urban location.

Taken as a whole, these findings suggest that Americans are watching energy developments closely. They expect that there will be many changes in the years ahead. They appear to be readying themselves for future changes and will not be caught entirely unprepared. Thus, the American energy future appears to be unfolding while our citizenry is alert to the fact of change and while many of them are ready to implement additional conserving behaviors.

How we adapt to the life ways the future brings will of course be a function of myriad variables and lies beyond the ability of any forecaster to predict. The general outlines of our potential adaptations have been sketched in different scenarios, however, and the questions they pose are clear. Will we, as Warren Johnson contends, muddle our way toward frugality in such a way as "to learn how to do things with our own hands again, how to pull communities back together, how to raise our children, and how to allow our elders a useful and agreeable life"? Or will we, as a *Business Week* reviewer contends, "never willingly" give up the "fruits of technological progress" nor our ability to produce "totally unexpected technological change" which may "make today's predictions of disaster seem absurd"? Or will we, as Roberto Vacca delineates, not find our tech-fixes for managing the energy transition? Will we instead find ourselves trapped in the steady disintegration of the technological age and the emergence of an era of Hobbesian war of each against each, in which only the predators survive, and all veneer of culture disappears in an age of war and revolution?

We as individuals, family members, members of neighborhoods and communities, and Americans are in some substantial part responsible for the energy future we shall live. We will be building that future in the years ahead, and we can shape it to substantial extent in assuring that it provides us adequacy and not shortfall. The building of a satisfactory energy future is one of the greatest challenges that confronts our community development processes in the years ahead.

SELF-HELP, VOLUNTARY ACTION, AND SELF-INTEREST: KEYS TO OUR ENERGY FUTURE

The energy future of the United States often appears to rest in the hands of a few remote decision makers, men who control the vast decision-making systems of federal government and multinational corporations. After all, it is the president and key congressional leaders who have the power to tax, or not to tax, the corporate explorers of oil and gas. It is they who can subsidize the development of synthetic fuels by the costly transformation of shale. It is they who will either maintain the international peace or steer our nation into war or a series of wars, which may strain both available supplies and the continuation of imported fuel supplies.

The leaders of the energy corporations will seek to use the great economic power of their industry to increase its level of profit by the extraction of as much oil and gas as possible, to be sold at the highest prices possible. In this effort they will be joined by many leaders of public utilities corporations, seeking to maintain the capacity of existing capital investments and to justify the added construction of nuclear facilities.

The election of Ronald Reagan appears to solidify the common front between a federal government committed to hard-path expansion and a monopolistic corporate sector dedicated to enhancing its already skyrocketing profits. In his acceptance speech for the Republican nomination for the presidency, Mr. Reagan said:

> Those who preside over the worst energy shortage in our history tell us to use less, so that we will run out of oil, gasoline, and natural gas a little more slowly. Well, now conservation is desirable, of course, but we must not waste energy. But conservation is not the sole answer to our energy needs.
>
> America must get to work producing more energy. The Republican program for solving economic problems is based on growth and productivity.
>
> Large amounts of oil and natural gas lay [sic] beneath our land and off our shores, untouched because the present administration seems to believe the American people would rather see more regulation, more taxes and more controls than more energy.
>
> Coal offers a great potential. So does nuclear energy produced under rigorous safety standards. It could supply electricity for thousands of industries and millions of jobs and homes. It must not be thwarted by a tiny minority opposed to economic growth which often finds friendly ears in regulatory agencies for its obstructionist campaigns.
>
> Now make no mistake. We will not permit the safety of our people or our environmental heritage to be jeopardized, but we are going to reaffirm that the economic prosperity of our people is a fundamental part of our environment.

Against this puissant union of big government and big business is there any chance for the development of energy coproduction on a community scale in the United States? Or, rather, is our energy future almost entirely to remain in the control of those committed to hard-path expansion, with all its risks of escalating prices and sudden shortfall?

At first blush, the combined forces of self-help, self-interest, and voluntary action may seem so puny as to be insignificant when set against the joint resolve of governmental and corporate elites. Yet these three forces may prove to be determinative.

For example, consider the following scenario on a possible future union of self-help and self-interest.

The technology of photovoltaic collection, having become widely available by 1990, is shown to generate electrical power at a rate below that provided by utility companies. Within another decade, a substantial proportion of the nation's wealthier home owners will avail themselves of this new energy source. Although this process of diffusion would have been more rapidly adopted had long-term, low-interest federal loans been made available, the self-interest of upper-income home owners, together with their resources, allows the introduction of a powerful renewable technology. Photovoltaics are used by upper-class home owners and within a generation trickle down to many homes of middle- and lower-class individuals, as increasing numbers of landlords convert their units and as increasing numbers of moderate-income home owners secure commercial loans to achieve the savings they see being reaped by their wealthier neighbors.

As photovoltaics spread through society, so does the preference for the small, gasoline-efficient automobile, the increasing application of insulation and energy conservation in the home, the limitation of energy use in personal transport, and a general achievement of the elimination of most of the 40 percent cushion of waste we presently expend.

These forms of energy-saving come to be reinforced by a vast network of energy self-help that emerges in the 1980s and burgeons in the 1990s. Groups of neighbors or friends join in "solar co-ops" in ever-expanding numbers, assisting each other in the weatherization of their homes, the installation of effective energy collectors, and the development of neighborhood energy collectors. Networks of these local cells coordinate organized car and van pools, not only to work but also to school, for shopping, and for recreational activities.

The development of this array of groups engaged in active energy conservation, furthermore, strengthens a national movement of energy coproducers and conservers. The power of these interlocked voluntary associations becomes recognized by political and corporate leaders alike. Elected officials are "targeted" for support or defeat by the emerging "solar majority" and come to recognize that it is only good politics to provide low-interest loans for solar conversion and outright subsidies for the retrofitting of homes of low-income persons. In this new political climate, a public policy of energy coproduction flourishes, embodied in a series of building codes, zoning ordinances, and national regulatory standards.

Long before they are mandated by government to provide such support, enterprising entrepreneurs corner much of the photovoltaics market. Utility companies themselves invest in such expenditures by home owners and buy back the surplus energy thereby generated as a way of returning a continuing gain to themselves to replace revenues lost in the decreasing use of their hard-energy consumables. Large energy corporations busy themselves diversifying their interests in renewable energy, buying out those of the new entrepreneurs that they can, and seeking to convert their processing of liquid fuels from mining and synfuels to the refining of grain alcohol and other renewable liquid fuels.

A fantasy? Perhaps; for the future cannot be precisely known. A possibility—but likely to arrive too slowly? Again, perhaps; for the American faith in hard-energy paths is strong. But impossible? By no means, especially in an era in which individual belief in the limits of government and corporation have never been greater and in which there is a renewed faith in individual initiative and community self-determination. The future need not belong to big government and big business united in the quest for the controlled profits of centralized energy. An alternative vision, as conservative as the founding image of American society and as firmly based as our traditions of consumer sovereignty and self-determination, can be developed by a generation of emerging entrepreneurs and community developers.

This vision rests upon two of our most powerful beliefs—individual self-interest and the right of the people to govern. Lawrence Goodwyn captures that vision well when he writes of American populism: "The Populists believed they could work together to be free individually. In their institutions of self-help, Populists developed and acted upon a crucial democratic insight: to be encouraged to surmount rigid cultural inheritances and to act with autonomy and self-confidence, individual people need the psychological support of other people."

It is such a vision that would underlie the emergence of a new solar majority. One by one its members are even now preparing for the rigors of hard-path shortfall, seeking to insulate themselves and their families from the dislocations of the next period of gasoline lines, oil shortages, and interruptions of natural gas flow, as well as from the price shock of natural gas deregulation and the continuing escalation in the prices of energy that have come to characterize even normal times.

Two by three by ten by hundreds and then thousands, it is they who may join with their neighbors in seeing the wisdom and necessity of the choice of coproduction. It is they who may well become the energy majority of the 1990s and beyond.

Epilogue: The Impact of Energy Transformation

MEASURING ATTITUDES AND BEHAVIOR

Works by social scientists customarily conclude with a chapter on future trends and possibilities, which extends their analysis of what has happened in the recent past to what might occur in the future. However, since the present volume has been largely concerned with the future, the conventional conclusion is obviously inappropriate.

Seizing the opportunity to do something different, I have chosen to conclude this volume with a set of comments and exercises designed to let readers assess the personal impact of possible urban energy futures on their own lives. This decision is made in the belief that the most critical determinant of our societal response to energy futures will rest in the choices, orientations, and attitudes of individual citizens. If, even in the event of precipitous energy dislocation, a viable energy future can be constructed, the willingness to act intelligently and responsibly in that future becomes an important factor, even more crucial than level of energy supply in determining the way we shall live.

Three exercises are presented for the reader's use. The first two assess the perception of energy transformation, its likelihood, and its magnitude. The third exercise assesses the reader's present energy behavior, his or her likely future behavior, the extent to which changes in energy patterns would affect the life style of the reader, and the reader's level of satisfaction or dissatisfaction with these

possible developments. Scoring methods are given at the ends of the
exercises. The results furnish indexes of attitudes and behavior.

The reader is invited to use the forms provided in a personal copy
of the book to record perceptions; readers of library copies are requested to photocopy the forms before completing them.

EXERCISE 1

HOW REAL IS THE ENERGY PROBLEM?

For each question place a check in the response category that most
closely approximates your present opinion.

1. Do you believe the energy problem is real?

_____ (a) Yes
_____ (b) I'm not sure
_____ (c) No (please proceed to question 3)

2. Is the energy problem created primarily by higher prices or by a
    decreasing availability of resources?

_____ (a) Higher prices
_____ (b) Both in combination
_____ (c) Decreasing availability of resources

(3-7) Do you believe that supplies of the following hard-energy
       sources will be increasing or decreasing over the next twenty
       years?

(a) Will increase	(b) Will stay about the same	(c) Will decrease
3. Coal		
4. Nuclear		
5. Oil (petroleum)		
6. Natural gas		
7. Synfuels		

8. Do you expect per capita energy availability in the United
    States to be greater or about the same in the year 2000?

_____ (a) Greater
_____ (b) About the same
_____ (c) Lesser

(9-15) How likely do you believe it is that the following events
       affecting energy supply will occur over the next decade?

(a)	(b)	(c)	(d)	(e)
Almost certain	Quite likely	Possible	Somewhat unlikely	Highly unlikely

9. An embargo of OPEC oil lasting more than three months

10. A war in the Mideast oil area destroying refineries and interrupting more than 10% of the world's imports

11. A continuing rise in world oil demand

12. A world war beginning in the oil areas

13. Shifts in overseas oil to nations unwilling to sell to the U.S.

14. Energy famines in the Third World leading to widespread loss of life

15. An accident at a nuclear power plant leading to loss of plant and permanent abandonment of surrounding land

16. What proportion of space heating and cooling need do you believe can be met in the United States from solar energy by the year 2000?

    _____ (a) Less than 10%
    _____ (b) Between 10 and 50%
    _____ (c) Over 50%

17. What word best expresses your view of the likely condition of American energy supplies in the year 2000?

    _____ (a) Opulent
    _____ (b) Sufficient
    _____ (c) Shortfall

In order to score your responses, give yourself points as indicated for each of the listed responses:

- Two points each for answers 1-c, 4-a, 5-a, 9-e, 10-d, 10-e, 11-e, 12-e, 13-e, 14-e, 15-e, 17-a
- One point each for answers 2-a, 6-a, 8-a, 9-d, 10-c, 11-d, 12-d, 13-d, 14-d, 15-d, 16-a.

Now sum your points. If your score is 16 or higher, you may be considered a hard-energy optimist. If your score is between 5 and 15, you are concerned about the adequacy of the hard-energy path. If your score is 4 or below, it would appear that you are a nonbeliever in the adequacy of the hard-energy path.

EXERCISE 2

PERCEPTIONS OF FUTURE ENERGY TRANSFORMATION

Instructions:

To assess your own perceptions of the dimensions of the coming energy transformation, if any, enter your predictions regarding the likelihood of the list of possible changes found below. For each possible change, place your estimate of its likelihood using a scale of 1 to 5 in which:

(1) means you are nearly certain that 50% or more of the population will be demonstrating the particular energy behavior indicated;

(2) means that you believe the behavior will quite likely be adopted by 50% or more of the population;

(3) means that you think there is about an even chance that the behavior will characterize 50% or more of the population;

(4) means that you find the possibilities quite unlikely to characterize 50% or more of the population; and

(5) means that you believe it is almost impossible that half the population will be behaving in the ways indicated.

Now for each of the energy behaviors listed below, assess the probability, in your own judgment, that they will characterize 50% of the United States population twenty years from now.

Twenty years from now, I expect
the likelihood that 50% or
more of the U.S. population
will engage in the following
behavior

1. Regularly ride to work on public
transportation in van pools or
car pools, or by walking or
bicycling

2. Almost never ride to and from
work as the sole passenger in a
private automobile

3. Travel less frequently by
airplane than at present

4. Drive an electric rather than
a gasoline-fueled automobile

5. Travel fewer miles by personal
automobile than at present

6. Have moved from one residence to
another with a primary goal of
locating within walking or
bicycling distance to work

7. Reside within walking distance
of schools and shopping
facilities

8. Have moved from one residence to
another with a primary goal of
generating excess electric power
for sale from backyard or rooftop collectors

9. Grow about half the fruits and
vegetables personally consumed
on a private or neighborhood
plot

10. Have fully winterized their
homes by means of weather
stripping, installation of storm
windows, caulking of windows,
addition of insulation, and
installation of flue dampers

11. Have installed a solar collector
for space and water heating

12. Reside in a home heated, at
least in part, by passive solar
design

13. Reside in a home heated and
     cooled by being located
     partially underground or covered
     by ground

14. Have closed off or do not heat
     two rooms in the house during
     the coldest months of the year

15. Live in a smaller home than
     present, but one that is less
     energy consuming

16. Keep home heating temperatures
     below 65° and limit home cooling
     temperatures to 78° and above

17. Actively practice energy
     conservation in everyday life

To score yourself on Exercise 2, simply add the numbers you have given in response to each item. Your score can be interpreted as follows:

- If your score is 40 or below, you believe that the United States will experience a profound transformation in energy use and behavior in the next two decades.

- If your score is between 41 and 60, you expect a partial transformation in the coming decades.

- If your score is 61 or above, you believe that any energy transformation the United States may experience will be limited in both its scope and scale.

Another way to score Exercise 2 is by totaling your scores on items 4, 8, 9, 11, 12, and 19. This will give us a measure of perceived solar energy transformation. A score of 15 or less indicates an expectation of massive solar transformation. A score between 16 and 20 indicates an expectation of substantial solar progress. And a score of 21 or above indicates a perception that the coming of solar transformation will be limited, at least in the decades ahead.

Table E.1

Percentages of U.S. Population Currently

Practicing Energy-Conserving Behaviors

BEHAVIOR	PERCENT OF POPULATION PRACTICING BEHAVIOR
1. Regularly ride to and from work on public transportation	8%
2. Almost never ride to and from work as sole passenger in auto	43%
3. Travel less frequently by airplane than at present	(Airplane traffic fell by 5% between 1979-1980)
4. Drive an electric automobile	0%
5. Travel fewer miles by personal automobile	(51% reported reducing driving in 1979)
6. Move from one residence to another with goal of reducing commuting distance	(No perceptible trend as of 1980)
7. Reside within walking distance of schools and shopping	Not available
8. Move to new residence with goal of generating excess electric power	(No perceptible trend as of 1980)
9. Grow half or more fruits/vegetables consumed	(During WW II, 20 million "Victory Gardens" produced 40% of our vegetables)
10. Have fully winterized home	Not available
11. Have installed solar collectors	Less than 1%
12. Reside in passive solar home	Less than 1%
13. Reside in earth-sheltered home	Less than 1%
14. Close off rooms in winter	48%
15. Live in smaller, less energy-consuming home	(No perceptible trend as of 1980)
16. Keep winter temperatures below 65°; summer above 78°	(65% report keeping setting below 68° in 1976)
17. Actively practice conservation	Not available

Sources (listed by items above):

1. On van pooling: Helen Sever, Presentation to National Conference on Volunteerism, Minneapolis (October 1980). On the other modes: George H. Gallup, ed., The Gallup Poll: Public Opinion 1979 (Wilmington, Del.: Scholarly Resources, Inc., 1980).
2. Center for Science in the Public Interest, 99 Ways to a Simple Lifestyle (Garden City, N.Y.: Anchor, 1977), p. 293.
3. News report.
4. Author's estimate.
5. Gallup, 1979.
6. Author's estimate.
8. Author's estimate.
9. Center for Science in the Public Interest, 99 Ways, p. 145.
11. Don Aitken, Speech to the Second Conference on Community Renewable Energy Systems, SERI, Seattle (September 3-5, 1980).
12. Author's estimate.
13. Author's estimate.
14. Bonnie Maas Morrison, Joanne Goodman Keith, and James J. Zuiches, "Impacts on Household Energy Consumption: An Empirical Study of Michigan Families," in C. T. Unseld et al., eds., Sociopolitical Effects of Energy Use and Policy, Supporting Paper 5, Study of Nuclear and Alternative Energy Systems (Washington, D.C.: National Academy of Sciences, 1979), p. 17.
15. Author's estimate, influenced by Michael deCourcy Hinds, "Despite a Trend Toward Conservation, New Homes Are Called Energy Sieves," The New York Times (December 28, 1980).
16. Morrison, "Impacts," p. 17.

Readers may now wish to add wrinkles of their own and create new exercises and scoring methods. Computations of perceptions of energy life in the year 2020 or 2050 may be developed and scored in the manner provided above. Comparisons with data available in 1980 on the various behaviors may be made by consulting Table E.1, which presents information relevant to the various energy-conserving actions.

Once one has grasped the magnitude of expected energy transformation, it is also useful to assess the impact the transformation is likely to have on one's own life. Here we shall use the same list of energy-related behaviors that were considered in the previous exercise. This time we ask four different questions. We begin with the present, with an assessment of current patterns of energy use and conservation. Then we move to assess the likely changes to be brought in the next two decades. Third, an effort is made to understand the magnitude of these changes on our life styles. And, finally, our general satisfaction or dissatisfaction with these potentialities is assessed.

To develop an understanding of his or her own likely energy transformation, then, the reader is asked to record responses to each of the four questions following the instructions in Exercise 3.

EXERCISE 3

PERSONAL ENERGY BEHAVIOR AND TRANSFORMATION

Instructions:

This is a four-part exercise. Each part employs the following list of energy behaviors. Pass through the list four times, each time using a different question and set of codes for your response.

First pass: Assessment of present behavior. Place a check by each item on the list that represents a current behavior of yours.

Second pass: Prediction of future behavior. Using the following five-point scale, indicate your prediction of the probability that, within the next twenty years, you will be engaging in any of the listed energy behaviors.

1) It is nearly certain that I will be doing this;
2) It is quite likely that I will be doing this;
3) There is an even chance I will be doing this;
4) There is a rather small chance that I will be doing this.
5) There is almost no possibility that I will be doing this.

Third pass: <u>Potential life style change</u>. Using the following five-point scale to indicate your judgment, score each of the energy-related behaviors in terms of the degree to which it represents a change from your own plans for a future life style:

1) It represents an enormous change;
2) It represents a fairly large change;
3) It represents a modest change;
4) It represents a rather small change;
5) It represents no change at all--I already do it.

Fourth pass: <u>Potential dissatisfaction or satisfaction</u>. Using the following five-point scale to indicate your response, score each of the energy-related behaviors in terms of the pleasure or displeasure you would feel if you engaged in that behavior. This time:

1) Enormous displeasure--I would do almost anything to avoid this situation;
2) Strong displeasure--I would do it only after trying most other ways of reducing energy use;
3) Neither clear pleasure nor displeasure--it would be acceptable to me;
4) Some pleasure--I would be happy to do it; and
5) Great pleasure--I would not only enjoy doing it but feel that it's the right thing to do.

	Present behavior	Future behavior	Potential life style change	Potential dissatis- faction
1. Regularly ride to and from work in a van pool or car pool, by public transportation or bicycle, or walk				
2. Almost never ride to and from work as the sole passenger in a private automobile				
3. Travel less frequently by airplane than ten years previously				
4. Drive an electric rather than a gasoline-fueled automobile				

5. Travel fewer miles by
    personal automobile than
    ten years previously

6. Have moved from one
    residence to another
    with a primary goal of
    locating within walking
    or bicycling distance to
    work

7. Reside within walking
    distance of schools and
    shopping facilities

8. Have moved from one
    residence to another
    with a primary goal of
    generating excess elec-
    tric power for sale from
    backyard or rooftop
    collectors

9. On a private or neigh-
    borhood plot, grow about
    half the fruits and
    vegetables personally
    consumed

10. Have fully winterized
    home by means of weather
    stripping, installation
    of storm windows,
    caulking of windows,
    addition of insulation,
    and installation of flue
    dampers

11. Have installed a solar
    collector for space and
    water heating

12. Reside in a home heated,
    at least in part, by
    passive solar design

13. Reside in a home heated
    and cooled by being
    located partially under-
    ground or covered by
    ground

14. Have closed off or don't
    heat two rooms in the
    house during the coldest
    months of the year

15. Live in a smaller home
    than previously but one
    that is less energy
    consuming

16. Keep home heating
    temperatures below 65°
    and limit home cooling
    temperatures to 78° and
    above

17. Actively practice energy
    conservation in everyday
    life

Four methods of scoring may be now used. The first will measure opinions on present conservation, the second on future conservation, the third on potential life style changes, and the fourth on future dissatisfaction.

To score for opinions on present conservation, count the number of checks in the first column. If your count is 7 or above, you are presently conserving energy in an active and widespread fashion. If your count is between 3 and 6, you are moderately active in conservation. If your score is 2 or below, you are not actively seeking to conserve energy at this time.

To score for opinions on future conservation, add the points of your responses in the second column. If they total less than 37, it is an indication that you anticipate full participation in a future of energy transformation. If your score falls between 37 and 53, it is an indication that you expect a considerable transformation in your energy-related behavior. And if your score is above 53, it would appear that you believe yourself to be largely protected from any coming energy transformation.

To score for views on potential life-style changes, add all the points of your responses in the third column. If your score is 27 or below, your life style will be greatly altered by energy shortfall. If your score is between 28 and 53, moderate changes in your life style would be introduced by energy shortfall. If your score is over 53, you are probably already living in an energy-conserving life style and can anticipate few additional changes in the event of energy shortfall.

Finally, to score responses on potential dissatisfaction, again total all points. If your score is 75 or above, you can take comfort in knowing that an energy-conserving future will not be unpleasant to you, but will fit well with your own vision of how life should be lived. If your score is between 46 and 74, you will be somewhat troubled by some changes in your life, but should adjust acceptably to a situation of energy shortfall. If your score is 45 or below, however, you are likely to be deeply troubled by the imposition of energy-short life ways.

TOWARD AN INDIVIDUAL PROFILE ON ENERGY

The energy indices resulting from the seven methods of scoring the exercises should now be arrayed together and their interrelationships considered. Table E.2 demonstrates the various possible outcomes. Certain patterns seem to be generally consistent with each other, while others suggest disparity. Easiest to identify are the energy ideologies identified in the first chapter. The believer in energy plenitude is the hard-energy optimist (I-C), expecting no, or at most a limited, energy transformation (2-C), perceiving limited solar development (2a-C), not actively conserving energy (3-C), perceiving himself or herself protected from energy transformation (4-C), and wide open to great alterations in life style (5-C) and profound dissatisfaction (6-C) in the event of energy shortfall. The believer in energy transformation, on the other hand, tends toward the polar position on the opposite side of the energy conservative, disbelieving in hard-energy sufficiency (I-A), expecting a profound energy transformation (2-A), seeing a massive shift to solar energy (2a-A), presently conserving energy (3-A), expecting to participate fully in energy transformation (4-A), moving toward a conserving life style (5-A), and welcoming the coming of the new energy-conserving ways (6-A).

Between the polar positions on each dimension stands the energy pragmatist, concerned about the coming energy transformation (1-B), expecting a partial transformation of energy behavior (2-B), anticipating significant progress in solar development and use (2a-B), engaging already in some conservation (3-B), expecting considerable personal transformation in energy use (4-B), anticipating moderate alterations in personal life styles (5-B), and preparing to adjust to these manageable uncertainties (6-B).

The reader will, of course, already have taken the opportunity to place himself or herself on the seven dimensions. While it is likely that many will land consistently on the types described in the preceding paragraphs, there will certainly be some who will find themselves in different patterns. For instance, it is certainly a reasonable position to expect hard-energy insufficiency (1-A) but to

Table E.2

Summary of Attitudes and Behavior

1. Reality of Energy Problem	2. Future Energy Transformation	2a. Perceived Solar Transformation	3. Present Conservation	4. Future Conservation	5. Potential Life-Style Change	6. Future Dissatisfaction
A. Non-Believer in Hard Energy	A. Expect Profound Transformation	A. Massive Solar	A. Active	A. Full Participation	A. Already Conserving	A. Welcomes
B. Concerned	B. Expect Partial Transformation	B. Solar Process	B. Moderate	B. Considerable Transformation	B. Moderate Alteration	B. Adjusts
C. Hard Energy Optimist	C. Expect Limited/No Transformation	C. Limited Solar	C. Inactive	C. Perceived Protection	C. Great Alteration	C. Is Disrupted

anticipate limited transformation to solar or conserving ways (2-C, 2a-C). Such an individual might also perceive considerable life-style changes and contemplate such an imbalanced future with concern and apprehension (4-B, 5-B, 6-C).

How we interpret our energy future and how we will feel living it also depend on the overall pattern of societal development. If we are fortunate to live in a good-luck future, whatever its energy base, we may well be happier than if a hard-luck future comes into being. The reader may want to return to the three scenarios presented in Chapter 3 and reflect on which seems most likely to emerge in the years ahead. An even more productive exercise would be to con- template what needs to be done to assure that a good-luck future will come into existence. What must each of us do to assure that such a future will be ours?

ENVOI

We are left with two questions: What should we do about our energy future? What will that energy future be?

The author chooses to leave the first question to the good sense of the reader. In a democracy, those policies are the wisest that reflect the careful thought of citizens. This book has been aimed to assist in the stimulation of such reflective consideration.

What will happen? The response must be even more indefinite. Our future is shared by billions of other persons whose choices and decisions will, along with our own, ultimately determine the future shape of our nation and world.

That awesome future stands before us and unfolds but a day at a time. For our energy choices, the range of the possible is broad, at least for the decade ahead. We live in a time of enormous uncer- tainty and great potential for disruption of established life ways and expectations.

All that is certain is we who now live are the stewards of our civilization for a few brief years and our choices will make some dif- ference on the future of that civilization. To that degree, we *do* choose the way we may live. Never has that margin of choice been more fateful. Unlike Pascal, we bet not on our immortal souls but on the very mortality of ourselves, our children, and their descendants until the end of earthly time.

Notes

CHAPTER 1

Pages 6–7
Sjoberg on the energy-poor city: Gideon Sjoberg, *The Preindustrial City: Past and Present* (New York: The Free Press, 1960), pp. 91–99, 104–105, 323.

Page 7
Roebuck on early coal mining in Britain: Janet Roebuck, *The Shaping of Urban Society: A History of City Forms and Functions* (New York: Charles Scribner's Sons, 1974), p. 77.

Mumford on the industrial city: Lewis Mumford, *The City in History: Its Origins, Its Transformations, and Its Prospects* (New York: Harcourt, Brace, Jovanovich, Inc., 1961), p. 46.

Page 8
Warner on the "walking city": Sam Bass Warner, *Streetcar Suburbs: The Process of Growth in Boston 1870–1900* (Cambridge, Mass.: Harvard University Press and MIT Press, 1962), pp. 16–17, 22.

Pages 8–9
On Robert Moses: see Robert A. Caro, *The Power Broker* (New York: Vintage, 1975). Other references in that string: John Keats, *The Crack in the Picture Window* (Boston: Houghton Mifflin, 1968); Scott Greer, *The Urban View* (New York: Oxford University Press, 1972); William H. Whyte, Jr., *The Last Landscape* (New York: Anchor, 1968); Robert Venturi and Denise Scott Brown, *Learning from Las Vegas* (Cambridge, Mass.: MIT Press, 1977).

Page 9
Berry on spread: Brian J. L. Berry, "The Geography of the United States in the Year 2000," in J. Friedmann and W. Alonso, eds., *Regional Policy: Readings in Theory and Applications* (Cambridge, Mass.: MIT Press, 1975), p. 132.

Pages 12-13
Bounty of energy supplied: George B. Dantzig and Thomas L. Saaty, *Compact City: A Plan for a Liveable Urban Environment* (San Francisco: W. H. Freeman, 1973), pp. 129-130.
Congressman (now Director of the Office of Management and Budget) Stockman on proven reserves: David A. Stockman, "The Wrong Way?: The Case Against a National Energy Policy," *The Public Interest* 53 (Fall 1978), pp. 11, 15.

Pages 12, 14
Denis Hayes, *Rays of Hope: The Transition to a Post-Petroleum World* (New York: W. W. Norton, 1977).

Page 14
Amory Lovins, *Soft Energy Paths: Toward a Durable Peace* (Cambridge, Mass.: Ballinger, 1977), pp. 38-39.
Barry Commoner, *The Politics of Energy* (New York: Random House, 1979).
Quotes from Denis Hayes, *Rays of Hope:* 80 percent of oil and gas supplies depleted, p. 48; nuclear technology unworkable, pp. 26-27; renewable sources, p. 155.

Pages 14-15
Lovins on soft technologies: *Soft Energy Paths,* pp. 38-39.

Page 15
Commoner on solar transition: *Politics of Energy,* p. 75.

Pages 15-16
Commoner's optimism: *Ibid.,* p. 82.

Page 16
Earl T. Hayes on the day of reckoning: Earl T. Hayes, "Energy Resources Available to the United States, 1985 to 2000," *Science* 203 (January 19, 1979), p. 233.

Earl T. Hayes on energy growth: *Ibid.*, p. 239.
Denis Hayes on inefficient buildings: *Rays of Hope*, p. 208.
David Stockman on energy quacks: "The Wrong Way?" pp. 40–41.

Page 17
Stockman on decontrol and dismantling: *Ibid.*, p. 40.

Page 19
Pascal presented his wager in his *Pensées*: Blaise Pascal, "Thoughts," in Monroe C. Beardsley, ed., *The European Philosophers from Descartes to Nietzsche* (New York: The Modern Library, 1960), pp. 100–136; the quotation is from p. 118.
    Oil and gas consumption cannot quintuple: Denis Hayes, *Rays of Hope*, p. 25.
    Sternlieb on the historical shift: George Sternlieb, "Forum—The Future is a Different United States," in Robert W. Burchell and David Listokin, eds., *Future Land Use: Energy, Environmental, and Legal Constraints* (New Brunswick, N.J.: Center for Urban Policy Research, 1975), p. 352.

CHAPTER 2

Pages 21–22
For a sampling of futurist approaches: Consult *The Futurist*, the publication of the World Futurist Society, P.O. Box 30369, Bethesda Branch, Washington, D.C. 20014.
    The works of Harman, Kahn, Roszak, and Janowitz are frequently cited in this chapter: Willis W. Harman, *An Incomplete Guide to the Future* (New York: W. W. Norton, 1979); Herman Kahn, *The Next 200 Years: A Scenario for America and the World* (New York: William Morrow, 1976); Theodore Roszak, *Person/Planet* (New York: Anchor, 1979); Morris Janowitz, *The Last Half-Century* (Chicago: University of Chicago Press, 1978). Another excellent futurist study is Gary Gappert, *Post-Affluent America: The Social Economy of the Future* (New York: New Viewpoints, 1979).
    The other books mentioned by Roszak are: Theodore Roszak, *The Making of a Counter-Culture* (Garden City, N.Y.: Doubleday, 1969); and *Where the Wasteland Ends* (Garden City, N.Y.: Doubleday, 1972).

Page 22

Roszak on other futurists: *Person/Planet,* p. 37.

Janowitz on futurology: *The Last Half-Century,* p. 546.

Kahn and Bruce-Briggs on normative futurology: Herman Kahn and Barry Bruce-Briggs, *Things to Come* (New York: Macmillan, 1972), pp. 245–246. My attention to this quote came from its citation by William Van Til in his *Secondary Education: School and Community* (Boston: Houghton Mifflin, 1978), p. 361.

One example, among many, of the use of the advocacy style by Roszak occurs in his discussion of the conventional assumption that "labor-saving" means "leisure-making" in technology. He writes: "Here, I adopt a radically different position, arguing that our personhood is realized in responsible work. Therefore, the true direction of progress is not to save labor, but to *preserve* it from indiscriminate technological advance: to preserve it, to make it whole, to make it real" (*Person/Planet,* p. 232).

Harman on transindustrial society: See *An Incomplete Guide to the Future,* p. 141.

Page 23

Kahn on postindustrial society: *The Next 200 Years,* p. 20.

Janowitz on the academic stance: *The Last Half-Century,* p. 558.

Sometimes futurists cast their work largely in quantitative terms and develop "models" in which a range of assumptions guides the hypothesized development of variables, and multitudinous "feedback loops" seek to simulate the interaction of these variables. Jay Forrester and the principals of the Club of Rome have pioneered these efforts, building national and world systems far into the twenty-first century and beyond. See Forrester's *World Dynamics* (Cambridge, Mass.: MIT Press, 1973); and Dennis Meadows et al., *The Limits to Growth* (New York: New American Library, 1974).

Other efforts are cast primarily in qualitative terms, though these often build on quantitative information as well. The thrust of these efforts is to try to understand futures as "gestalts," or consistent wholes. Harman, a primary practitioner of this school, explains it by noting that there are six main steps to this method: understand continuity; seek for self-consistency; identify similarities among social systems; discover cause-effect relationships; chart holistic trends; and be aware of the goals societies are seeking (*An Incomplete Guide to the Future,* pp. 10–14). Kahn's approach is similar in method to Harman's.

Page 24

On nuclear subsidies in the Reagan approach: Robert Stobaugh and Daniel Yergin note that "in view of the numerous deferrals and cancellations" in nuclear plant construction over recent years, and "the probable effects of the accident at Harrisburg," even "modest growth" in nuclear power generation "can by no means be considered a sure thing." *Energy Future: Report of The Energy Project at the Harvard Business School* (New York: Random House, 1979), p. 111.

Page 25

On fusion's prospects: *The New York Times* reported on January 13, 1980, that energy release from the $25 million Shiva fusion machine at the Lawrence Livermore Laboratory fell short of original predictions of its output by a factor of 10,000.

Page 26

On the role of plausibility, probability, and preferability in futures study: See Roy Amara, "The Futures Field: Searching for Definitions and Boundaries," *The Futurist* 14 (February 1981), pp. 25–29.

Parsons on the social system: Talcott Parsons, "On the Concept of Political Power," in R. Bendix and S. M. Lipset, eds., *Class, Status, and Power: Social Stratification in Comparative Perspective,* second edition (New York: The Free Press, 1966), pp. 240–265.

Page 27

In discussing inflation, reference will repeatedly be made to its relation to income growth. Technically, it is "stagflation" that will be discussed, as it is the hidden redistribution of income occasioned by inflation, in relation to income growth, that has the broadest societal implications for conflict and change. See Janowitz, *The Last Half-Century,* p. 256; and Lester C. Thurow, *The Zero-Sum Society: Distribution and the Possibilities for Economic Change* (New York: Basic Books, 1980), ch. 3.

The degree to which price inflation has recently exceeded wage increases, if at all, is a matter of varying interpretation. The Consumer Price Index (CPI) is in wide disrepute as a measure of inflation because of its own inflation by rises in housing prices and mortgage rates, and will be replaced by 1985 as the official societal measure of inflation. In 1979, for example, the CPI increased by 12.6 percent while the Commerce Index, which reflects rents rather than home-buying costs, advanced by 9.8 percent. Both exceeded the rise of net income for that year, however, which advanced by 8.7 percent.

Another perspective, not at all inconsistent with the above, is provided by Gar Alperovitz and his colleagues at the Exploratory Project for Economic Alternatives, who note that inflation hits low- and moderate-income persons more severely than those of greater means. This results from the fact that the inflation rate for necessities (food, shelter, health care, energy) has risen at 7.5 percent per year between 1971 and 1976, while the price of non-necessities increased at 5 percent per year. They also note that during the first half of 1978 food prices rose at an annual rate of 18 percent, fuel prices 15 percent, mortgage interest rates 18 percent, and hospital costs 9 percent—all in excess of that year's rise in the CPI of 7.6 percent (Consumers Opposed to Inflation in the Necessities, "Inflation Isn't a Natural Disaster: It's Caused by People Who Profit from It" [Washington, D.C., 1979]), p. 2.

The Wall Street Journal, approaching the problem from another direction, assures its readers that "inflation doesn't affect everybody anywhere near equally, and the chances are good that your own personal-expense inflation rate runs manageably lower than the current increase" in the CPI (Donald Moffitt, "Your Own Inflation Rate May Not Be as High as the Official Figure: Here's How to Find Out," *The Wall Street Journal,* December 3, 1979, p. 44).

For a discussion of the variety of anti-inflation policies, see Thurow, *The Zero-Sum Society,* pp. 61–74.

The concept of the "planning system": Galbraith defines the planning system as that part of the economy in which "the firm wins its control over prices automatically and with no public fanfare merely by being large." The remainder of the economy is identified as the "market system," in which those "who want stabilization of their prices or control of their supply must act collectively or get the assistance of the government." John Kenneth Galbraith, *Economics and the Public Purpose* (New York: New American Library, 1975), p. 49.

Page 28

Safire on meltdown: William Safire, "Economy in Meltdown," *The New York Times* (October 8, 1979).

Cornish on the coming crisis: Edward Cornish, "The Great Depression of the 1980s: Could it Really Happen?" *The Futurist* 13 (October 1979), pp. 353–380.

Pages 28–29
The optimistic scenario of the Joint Economic Committee appears to be based on assumptions so rosy as to be unrealistic to this writer and will therefore receive no consideration in this analysis. The computer-based research of the committee, nevertheless, is solid and worthy of serious attention. See Joint Economic Committee, Congress of the United States, *The U.S. Economy in the 1980s* (Washington, D.C.: Government Printing Office, 1979).

Page 29
Silk on low growth: Leonard Silk, "Higher Costs, Slower Growth Will Compel, Finally, Tough Choices," *The New York Times* (December 30, 1979). Other quotes from this article follow on subsequent pages of this chapter.

Pages 29–30
The quotes from Ernst, Ginzberg, Rosow, Freeman, and Weber are from R. C. Longworth and Bill Neikirk, "What Next? A Closed Door is Likely for All But the Very Best," *The Philadelphia Inquirer* (November 18, 1979).

Page 30
Janowitz: *The Last Half-Century*, p. 253. Roszak: *Person/Planet*, p. 211.
On the concentration of economic assets: See Galbraith, *Economics and the Public Purpose*, p. 43.

Page 31
Schochet on corporate social responsibility: Gordon Schochet, "Social Responsibility, Profits, and the Public Interest," *Society* 16 (March/April 1979), pp. 24, 26.

Page 32
The data on the distribution of income and wealth are taken from Lester Thurow, *The Zero-Sum Society*, ch. 7.

Page 36
Wolfe's statement was made in "The 'Me' Decade and the Third Great Awakening," *New York* (August 23, 1976).
Harman's material is presented in *An Incomplete Guide to the Future*, ch. 2.

Page 37
Yankelovich on the embryonic ethic: Daniel Yankelovich, "New Rules in American Life: Searching for Self-Fulfillment in a World Turned Upside Down," *Psychology Today* 15 (April 1981), p. 85. A fuller statement is found in the same author's *New Rules: Searching for Self-Fulfillment in a World Turned Upside Down* (New York: Random House, 1981).

Ferguson and Toffler: Marilyn Ferguson, *The Aquarian Conspiracy: Personal and Social Transformation in the 1980s* (Los Angeles: J. P. Tarcher, 1980); Alvin Toffler, *The Third Wave* (New York: Morrow, 1980).

Trecker on demographic futures: Harleigh Trecker, "Crucial Environmental Factors in the 1980s: Implications for Volunteerism," in Wayne D. Rydberg and Linda J. Peterson, eds., *A Look at the Eighties: Crucial Environmental Factors Affecting Volunteerism* (Appleton, Wis.: Aid Association for Lutherans, 1980).

Page 39
Molitor on information technologies: Graham T. T. Molitor, "The Information Society: The Path to Post-Industrial Growth," *The Futurist* 15 (April 1981), pp. 24–25.

Page 41
Madron on political futures: Thomas Wm. Madron, "Political Parties in the 1980s," *The Futurist* 13 (December 1979), pp. 465–476.

Page 42
Janowitz: *The Last Half-Century,* p. 538.

Page 43
Data on welfare expenditures are taken from U.S. Department of Health and Human Services, Social Security Administration, "Research and Statistics Note 4" (June 4, 1981), Table 1.

Page 44
Millionaires as senators: "New Data Show Richest Senator is Either Heinz, Danforth, or Pell," *The New York Times* (May 21, 1981).

Page 45
Etzioni on the "active society": Amitai Etzioni, *The Active Society* (New York: The Free Press, 1968).

Charles E. Lindblom of Yale is probably the most distinguished scholar to warn of the impact of corporate control. See his *Politics and Markets* (New York: Basic Books, 1977).

The failures of pluralism are also discussed by Sheldon Wolin, *Politics and Vision* (Boston: Little, Brown, 1960).

Page 46
On the distinction between "voluntarism" and "volunteerism": See Jon Van Til, "In Search of Volunt...ism," *Volunteer Administration* 12 (Summer 1979), pp. 8–20.

CHAPTER 3

Page 49
On modern society as a zero-sum enterprise: See Lester C. Thurow, *The Zero-Sum Society: Distribution and the Possibilities for Economic Change* (New York: Basic Books, 1980).

Page 56
Energy Policy Project of the Ford Foundation, *A Time to Choose: America's Energy Future* (Cambridge, Mass.: Ballinger, 1974).

Workshop on Alternative Energy Strategies, *Energy: Global Prospects 1985–2000* (New York: McGraw-Hill, 1977).

Friends of the Earth: John S. Steinhart et al., *Pathway to Energy Sufficiency: The 2050 Study* (San Francisco: Friends of the Earth, 1979).

The author of this book: Jon Van Til, "Spatial Form and Structure in a Possible Future: Some Implications of Energy Shortfall for Urban Planning," *Journal of the American Planning Association* 45 (July 1979), pp. 318–329.

Committee on Nuclear and Alternative Energy Systems, National Research Council, National Academy of Sciences, *Energy in Transition 1985–2010* (San Francisco: W. H. Freeman, 1980).

Page 57
In deriving the last two scenarios, the author has tried to make predictions consistent with the thrust of the Ford predictions and with the hypothesized elasticity of the major types of energy use. The Ford predictions are among the most optimistic in recent years regarding the future availability of energy supply. Following the models

of the Workshop on Alternative Energy Strategies would have led to even more stringent scenarios. Reliance on the Ford assumptions assures that the implications of the energy-scarce scenarios are conservative predictions from the perspective of energy shortfall.

Page 58
Dantzig and Saaty on energy savings: George B. Dantzig and Thomas L. Saaty, *Compact City: A Plan for a Liveable Urban Environment* (San Francisco: W. H. Freeman, 1973), pp. 80, 83.

Krenz on energy design: Jerrold Krenz, *Energy: From Opulence to Sufficiency* (New York: Hemisphere/Praeger, 1980).

Owen Phillips, *The Last Chance Energy Book* (Baltimore: Johns Hopkins University Press, 1979).

Robert Stobaugh and Daniel Yergin, eds., *Energy Future: Report of the Energy Project at the Harvard Business School* (New York: Random House, 1979).

Paolo Soleri, *Arcology: The City in the Image of Man* (Cambridge, Mass.: MIT Press, 1969).

Glen Small, "Land in the Sky: Vision of a Megastructure," *The Futurist* 11 (June 1977), pp. 150–156.

Percival Goodman on architectural curiosities: Percival Goodman, *The Double E* (Garden City, N.Y.: Anchor Press, 1977), pp. 8–9.

Page 63
Brower on the shrinking of the unthinkable: David R. Brower, preface to Steinhart et al., *Pathway to Energy Sufficiency*, p. 4.

Friends of the Earth scenarios: Steinhart et al., *Pathway to Energy Sufficiency*, pp. 14–16.

The Committee on Nuclear and Alternative Energy Systems summarizes its scenarios: *Energy in Transition*, p. 9.

Page 66
The Committee on Nuclear and Alternative Energy Systems on conservation: *Ibid.*, pp. 92–93.

Global 2000 Report on world energy supplies: Council on Environmental Quality and Department of State, *The Global 2000 Report to the President* (Washington, D.C.: Government Printing Office, 1980), vol. 2, p. 171.

Pages 66–67
Global 2000 Report on implications for the U.S.: *Ibid.*, p. 175.

Page 67
The Exxon scenario is found in: *Energy Outlook 1980–2000* (Houston: Exxon Co., 1979).

Pages 67–68
Resources for the Future on supply and price levels: A Study Group Administered by Resources for the Future, *Energy: The Next Twenty Years* (Cambridge, Mass.: Ballinger, 1979), p. 113.

Page 68
Resources for the Future on energy shortfall: *Ibid.,* pp. 7–8.
Resources for the Future on energy optimism: *Ibid.,* p. 7.
Bartlett and Steele on energy anarchy: Donald L. Bartlett and James B. Steele, "Energy Anarchy: The More We Use, the More We Have," *The Philadelphia Inquirer* (December 7, 1980), p. 16-A. Citing as their source the *Inquirer's* projection of government and industry data, the writers find that the United States possesses resources in the following oil equivalences: natural gas, 290 billion barrels; crude oil, 140 billion barrels; shale oil, 1,310 billion barrels; geopressured methane, 4,150 billion barrels; coal, 5,120 billion barrels.
For another statement of what W. Jackson Davis has called the "cornucopian" perspective: See Julian Simon, *The Ultimate Resource* (Princeton, N.J.: Princeton University Press, 1981).

Page 69
The Rand study: Douglas Martin, "New Study Is Pessimistic on Nation's Oil Potential," *The New York Times* (April 12, 1981).

Pages 69–70
Parisi's article: Anthony J. Parisi, "Hard Times for Nuclear Power," *The New York Times Magazine* (April 12, 1981), pp. 36ff.

CHAPTER 4

Page 71
Kevin Lynch, *The Image of the City* (Cambridge, Mass.: MIT Press, 1960).

Page 72
Burgess on the circular zone theory: Ernest W. Burgess, "The Growth of the City," in Robert E. Park, Ernest W. Burgess, and

Roderick W. McKenzie, eds., *The City* (Chicago: University of Chicago Press, 1925), pp. 50–51.

Maurice R. Davie, "The Pattern of Urban Growth," in G.P. Murdock, ed., *Studies in the Science of Society* (New Haven: Yale University Press, 1938), pp. 131–161.

Homer Hoyt, *The Structure and Growth of Residential Neighborhoods in American Cities* (Washington, D.C.: Federal Housing Association, 1939).

Chauncy D. Harris and Edward L. Ullman, "The Nature of Cities," *Annals of the American Academy of Political and Social Science* 242 (November 1945).

Page 74

Wurster on urban form: Catherine Bauer Wurster, "The Form and Structure of the Future Urban Complex," in Lowdon Wingo, Jr., ed., *Cities and Space* (Baltimore: Johns Hopkins Press for Resources for the Future, Inc., 1963), and in Eli Chinoy, ed., *The Urban Future* (New York: Lieber-Atherton, 1973).

David M. Gordon, "Class Struggle and the Stages of American Urban Development," in D. C. Perry and A. J. Watkins, eds., *The Rise of the Sunbelt Cities* (Beverly Hills, Calif.: Sage, 1977).

Page 76

The reader might wish to contrast the present description of Los Angeles with Ralph Thomlinson's: See Ralph Thomlinson, *Urban Structure: The Social and Spatial Character of Cities* (New York: Random House, 1969), pp. 300–301.

Page 79

Population by house type in Los Angeles and Philadelphia: In the Philadelphia Standard Metropolitan Statistical Area, more than 66 percent of the households live in single-family homes, while in Los Angeles, the proportion is 60 percent. However, half of the single-family homes in Philadelphia are attached to a neighbor's house, while only 4 percent are attached in Los Angeles (U.S. Department of Commerce, Bureau of Census, *1970 Census of Housing, Housing Characteristics for States, Cities and Counties,* Table 39).

Page 80

Robert E. Park on urban ecology: Robert E. Park, "Human Ecology," *American Journal of Sociology* 42 (July 1936), pp. 1–15.

Louis Wirth and the city: Louis Wirth, "Urbanism as a Way of Life," *American Journal of Sociology* 44 (July 1938), pp. 1–23.

On scale as a correlate of urbanization and modernization: See Scott Greer, *The Emerging City: Myth and Reality* (New York: The Free Press, 1962), ch. 2; Chinoy, *The Urban Future*, 1973, Introduction; Jean Gottman, *Megalopolis* (New York, The Twentieth Century Fund, 1961); C. A. Doxiadis and T. B. Douglass, *The New World of Urban Man* (Philadelphia: Church Press, 1965), ch. 3.

Page 81
On the continuation of increasing scale: See York Willbern, "The Transformation of the Urban Community," in Chinoy, ed., *The Urban Future*, pp. 23–41; John Friedmann and John Miller, "The Urban Field," in Chinoy, ed., *The Urban Future*, pp. 73–94; Herman Kahn and A. J. Wiener, "The Next Thirty-three Years: A Framework for Speculation," *Daedalus* 96 (Summer 1967), pp. 705–732; Brian J. L. Berry, "The Geography of the United States in the Year 2000," in J. Friedmann and W. Alonso, eds., *Regional Policy* (Cambridge, Mass.: MIT Press, 1975), pp. 106–136; Barry Bruce-Briggs, *The Future of Housing and Urban Development Policy* (Croton-on-Hudson, N.Y.: Hudson Institute, 1972); and Anthony Downs, "Forum – The Future Is Demographic Change," in R. W. Burchell and D. Listokin, eds., *Future Land Use: Energy, Environmental and Legal Constraints* (New Brunswick, N.J.: Center for Urban Policy Research, 1975).

Friedmann and Miller on the urban field: See "The Urban Field," p. 78.

Page 83
Population changes between 1970 and 1977: U.S. Department of Commerce, Bureau of the Census, Current Population Reports, Series P-25, No. 810, "Estimates of the Population of Counties and Metropolitan Areas: July 1, 1976 and 1977," (Washington, D.C.: Government Printing Office, 1979), Tables 1, 2, 5, 6, 7.

Pages 83, 85
Berry on counterurbanization: Brian J. L. Berry, "Urbanization and Counterurbanization in the United States," *Annals of the American Academy of Political and Social Science* 541 (September 1980), p. 16.

Page 85
Charles L. Leven, ed., *The Mature Metropolis* (Lexington, Mass.: D. C. Heath, 1978).

Dillman on the population turnaround: Don A. Dillman, "Residential Preferences, Quality of Life, and the Population Turnaround," *American Journal of Agricultural Economics* 61 (December 1979), p. 965.

Pages 85–86
Employment comparisons between 1948 and 1972: Arthur P. Solomon, "City and Suburb: Past, Present, and Future," in Arthur P. Solomon, ed., *The Prospective City* (Cambridge, Mass.: MIT Press, 1980), p. 7.

Page 86
Haren and Holling on timing of job increase: Claude D. Haren and Ronald W. Holling, "Industrial Development in Nonmetropolitan America: A Locational Perspective," in Ronald E. Lonsdale and H. L. Seyler, eds., *Nonmetropolitan Industrialization* (Washington, D.C.: V. W. Winston and Sons, 1979), pp. 13–45.

Black on suburban job loss: J. Thomas Black, "The Changing Economic Role of Central Cities," in Solomon, ed., *The Prospective City*, p. 102.

McKenzie on Northeastern recovery: Richard B. McKenzie, *Restrictions on Business Mobility: A Study in Political Rhetoric and Economic Reality* (Washington, D.C.: American Enterprise Institute for Public Policy Research, 1979), pp. 34–35.

McKenzie on birth and death rates of firms: *Ibid.*, pp. 38–39.

Page 87
Garn and Ledebur on urban distress: Harvey A. Garn and Larry Clinton Ledebur, "The Economic Performance and Prospects of Cities," in Solomon, ed., *The Prospective City*, pp. 204–257.

Page 88
Garn and Ledebur on economic and fiscal distress: *Ibid.*, p. 206.

James on revitalization: Franklin J. James, "The Revitalization of Older Urban Housing and Neighborhoods," in Solomon, ed., *The Prospective City*, pp. 154–155.

Page 89
Laska and Spain on revitalization: Shirley Laska and Daphne Spain, eds., *Back to the City? The Making of a Movement* (New York: Pergamon, 1980), p. xx. See also: Michael H. Lang, *Gentrification Amidst Urban Decline: Strategies for America's Older Cities* (Cambridge, Mass.: Ballinger, 1982).

Kahn and Frieden on urban futures: Quoted in Robert Reinhold, "Scholars Take Optimistic View of Energy Problems," *The New York Times* (July 5, 1979).

Page 90

Kasarda on the footloose economy: Quoted in John Herbers, "Experts Do Not Expect Energy Problems to Halt Population Shift Away from Cities," *The New York Times* (June 9, 1980). Kasarda's was one of a series of papers presented to a two-day symposium held by the President's Commission for a National Agenda for the Eighties. Later in 1980, considerable controversy was stirred by the rather uncritical acceptance by that commission of expanded growth in the Sunbelt and continuing attrition of the nation's older Northeastern and North-Central cities. See President's Commission for a National Agenda for the Eighties, *Urban America in the Eighties: Perspectives and Prospects* (Washington, D.C.: Government Printing Office, 1980). For a critical analysis of this position, see Timothy K. Barnekov, Daniel Rich, and Robert Warren, "The New Privatism, Federalism, and the Future of Urban Governance: National Urban Policy in the 1980s," *Journal of Urban Affairs* 3 (Fall 1981), pp. 1–14.

Keyes on energy transition: Dale L. Keyes, "The Future of Energy on Future Patterns of Urban Development," in Solomon, *The Prospective City*, p. 322.

Keyes on gains in income and rises in energy prices: *Ibid.*, p. 323.

Burch on easy answers: Quoted in Reinhold, *The New York Times* (July 5, 1979).

Page 91

On scale as a variable: This perspective is consonant with what Riley Dunlap and his colleagues have called the "ecological paradigm." See Riley E. Dunlap, "Paradigmatic Change in Social Science: The Decline of Human Exceptionalism and the Emergence of an Ecological Paradigm," *American Behavioral Scientist* 24 (September/October 1980); William R. Catton, Jr., and Riley E. Dunlap, "A New Ecological Paradigm for Post-Exuberant Sociology," in *Ibid.*

CHAPTER 5

Page 93

On the structure of energy itself, the following are most useful: Jerrold Krenz, *Energy: Conversion and Utilization* (Boston: Allyn and

Bacon, 1977); Jerrold Krenz, *Energy: From Opulence to Sufficiency* (New York: Hemisphere/Praeger, 1980).

Page 95
On the generation of electrical power: The conventional power plant loses over two-thirds of the energy sources it employs in heat and transmission losses, while producing a form of power (electricity) that is often ill-suited to the household uses to which it is put. See *Ibid.*

Page 97
On energy developments in Europe, the long quote is from: C. I. Jackson, *Human Settlements and Energy: An Account of the ECE Seminar on the Impact of Energy Considerations on the Planning and Development of Human Settlements, Ottawa, Canada, 3–14 October 1977* (Oxford: Published for the United Nations by Pergamon Press, 1978), pp. 38–39.

Page 98
Work by Lovins and Commoner was discussed in Chapter 1. Lawrence Solomon's major contribution is his *Energy Shock: After the Oil Runs Out* (Toronto: Doubleday Canada Limited, 1980).
Davis on resource exhaustion: W. Jackson Davis, *The Seventh Year* (New York: W. W. Norton, 1979), p. 41.
Davis on the last barrel: *Ibid.,* p. 42.

Page 99
Lovins on the coming water shortage: Comments at the Second Conference on Community Renewable Energy Systems, sponsored by the Solar Energy Research Institute and held in Seattle (September 3–5, 1980).
Richard J. Barnet, *The Lean Years* (New York: Simon and Schuster, 1980).
Jeremy Rifkin, *Entropy* (New York: Viking, 1980).
Vacca on the coming dark age: Roberto Vacca, *The Coming Dark Age* (Garden City, N.Y.: Doubleday, 1973), p. 179.
Vacca on the tools of survival: *Ibid.,* p. 213.

Page 100
Williams on American values: Robin M. Williams, Jr., *American Society* (New York: Knopf, 1965).
On the good behavior of lower-income Americans: See Robert E.

Lane, *Political Ideology* (New York: The Free Press, 1962).

Sorokin on sensate society: See Pitirim A. Sorokin, *The Crisis of Our Age* (New York: E. P. Dutton, 1941).

Toynbee on universal religion: Arnold T. Toynbee, *A Study of History*, abridged by D. C. Somervell (New York: Oxford University Press, 1946), vol. 2, p. 380.

Willis W. Harman, *An Incomplete Guide to the Future* (New York: W. W. Norton, 1979).

Page 101

Fels and Munson on transportation futures: Margaret Fulton Fels and Michael J. Munson, "Energy Thrift in Urban Transportation: Options for the Future," in Robert H. Williams, ed., *The Energy Conservation Papers* (Cambridge, Mass.: Ballinger, 1975), pp. 7–104.

Subcommittee report: Subcommittee on the City, Committee on Banking, Finance, and Urban Affairs, House of Representatives, 96th Congress, Second Session, *Compact Cities: Energy Savings Strategies for the Eighties* (Washington, D.C.: Government Printing Office, 1980), pp. 5–6.

Subcommittee on urban energy use: *Ibid.*, p. 13.

Page 104

Burton on spatial consequences of energy crisis: Dudley J. Burton, "Energy and Urban Form," in Gary A. Tobin, ed., *The Changing Structure of the City: What Happened to the Urban Crisis*, volume 16 of *Urban Affairs Annual Reviews* (Beverly Hills, Calif.: Sage, 1979), pp. 204–205. See also: John M. Wardell and C. Jack Gilchrist, "The Distribution of Population and Energy in Nonmetropolitan Areas: Confluence and Divergence," *Social Science Quarterly* 61 (December 1980), pp. 566–580.

On shortfall: It should be noted that other urban futurists have not envisaged such a possibility. Williams, Kruvant, and Newman, for example, write of city futures in three scenarios: "business as usual," "incentive-mandates," and "acute shortage." Their first two scenarios involve "no serious shortages," and the second differs from the first in that it is characterized by a "rapid and sustained price increase." Only their acute-shortage scenario involves "constricted supply." However, it is viewed "as a short-range phenomenon with some long-term reduction in energy consumption," which will merge with the second scenario as "society adapts to and learns to live with such a shortage."

Williams, Kruvant, and Newman thus do not deal directly with the problem of long-term adaptation to serious shortfall. Their second scenario does imply a number of major shifts in directions toward energy conservation in the home, density and intensity of land use, and shifts to public transportation. In none of their scenarios do they foresee a major shift in property values, job location, or changes in distance to work, although they do foresee "considerable development of all kinds of transportation/employment nodes in the suburbs."

The Williams-Kruvant-Newman model is based on a narrower and more salutary range of energy-supply options than Burton's analysis and that of the author of this book. It excludes from consideration what it recognizes as "another possibility—society does not adapt to acute shortage and the economy grinds to a halt." It also appears to overlook the position of endemic shortfall that requires substantial structural change for successful adaptation. Quotes from John S. Williams, Jr., William Kruvant, and Dorothy Newman, "Metropolitan Impacts of Alternative Energy Futures," in C. T. Unseld et al., eds., *Sociopolitical Effects of Energy Use and Policy,* Supporting Paper 5, Study of Nuclear and Alternative Energy Systems (Washington, D.C.: National Academy of Sciences, 1979), pp. 37–77.

Page 105

Doubling up of households: Pollster Albert Sindlinger found 600,000 fewer households in November 1980 than in July of the same year. He attributed this disappearance to the squeeze of inflation and recession. *Business Week* (December 8, 1980).

Meier on life styles in energy-short New York: Richard L. Meier, "Less Is More in Megalopolis," Working Paper 265, Institute of Urban and Regional Development (Berkeley: University of California, 1976), pp. 22–23.

Meier on lessons from the Third World: "A Stable Urban Ecosystem," *Science* 192 (June 4, 1976), p. 965.

Page 106

Business Week review: Michael G. Sheldrick, "Watching the World Run Out of Resources," *Business Week* (September 8, 1980), p. 12.

Page 107

Keyes on energy savings: Dale L. Keyes, "Land Use and Energy Conservation: Is There a Linkage to Exploit?" in R. J. Burby and A. F. Bell, eds., *Energy and the Community* (Cambridge, Mass.: Ballinger, 1978), p. 69.

Crane on energy savings: D. A. Crane, "Energy and Urban Living," in *Energy and the Quality of Life* (Houston, Tex.: Energy Institute of University of Houston and Rice University, 1976), p. 5.

Keyes on the limits of spatial transformation: Dale L. Keyes, in Arthur P. Solomon, ed., *The Prospective City* (Cambridge, Mass.: MIT Press, 1980).

Peterson and Hempel on decentralization: David L. Peterson and L. C. Hempel, "Settlement Patterns in the Post-Industrial Society: Redefining Urban and Rural." Paper presented to the Western Social Science Association (April 1979), abstract.

T. K. Bradshaw and Edward Blakely, *Rural Communities in Advanced Industrial Society: Development and Developers* (New York: Praeger, 1979).

Page 108

Van der Ryn on suburban agriculture: Sim Van der Ryn, "Ecotopia Now: Utopia Brought Down to Earth," *New Age* 26 (March 1979), p. 26.

Burton on decentralization: Dudley J. Burton, in Tobin, ed., *The Changing Structure of the City,* pp. 217–218.

An additional and fascinating consideration of the impact of changing transportation patterns: Samuel K. Klausner, "Forty Years in the Energy Desert: Life Styles in a Changing Environment," *The Forensic Review* 49 (August 1975).

A United Nations seminar: See Jackson, ed., *Human Settlements and Energy.*

The New York Times on the 1980s: See *The New York Times* (December 30, 1979).

On energy opulence versus sufficiency: See Krenz, *Energy: From Opulence to Sufficiency.*

Page 109

Zucchetto on energy studies: James Zucchetto, "Energy and Human Settlement Patterns," paper presented at the North American Meetings of the Regional Science Association, Milwaukee (November 1980).

Page 110

On the problem of increasing coal production: See Barry Commoner, *The Politics of Energy* (New York: Random House, 1979); and Carroll L. Wilson, *Coal — Bridge to the Future: Report to the World Coal Study* (Cambridge, Mass.: Ballinger, 1981).

On the tenuous future of the nuclear industry: See Robert Stobaugh and Daniel Yergin, eds., *Energy Future: Report of the Energy Project at the Harvard Business School* (New York: Random House, 1979), ch. 5. *The New York Times* reported on March 16, 1980 that since 1977 two new nuclear reactors have been ordered in the United States while prior orders for thirty-eight reactors have been cancelled. Three completed reactors were unplugged in this period, and sixty-seven remain in operation.

Lovins on centralizing energy: Amory Lovins, *Soft Energy Paths: Toward a Durable Peace* (Cambridge, Mass.: Ballinger, 1977), p. 55.

CHAPTER 6

Page 118
On the distribution of persons by social class in different community types: See John Fine, Norval D. Glenn, and J. Kenneth Months, "The Residential Segregation of Occupational Groups in Central Cities and Suburbs," *Demography* 8 (1971), pp. 91–101.

Page 120
On the possibility that aspiring urban residents might organize collectively: See Jon Van Til, "Citizen Participation in Neighborhood Transformation: A Social Movements Approach," *Urban Affairs Quarterly* 15 (June 1980), pp. 439–452.

Page 121
Friends of the Earth on the Year 2050: William Steinhart et al., *Pathway to Energy Sufficiency: The 2050 Study* (San Francisco: Friends of the Earth, 1979), p. 21.

Page 122
Friends of the Earth on urban agriculture: *Ibid.,* pp. 26–27.

Leven on the multinucleated metropolis: Charles Leven, "Economic Maturity in the Metropolis' Evolving Physical Form," in Gary A. Tobin, ed., *The Changing Structure of the City: What Happened to the Urban Crisis,* volume 16 of *Urban Affairs Annual Reviews* (Beverly Hills, Calif.: Sage, 1979), pp. 21–44; and Charles Leven, ed., *The Mature Metropolis* (Lexington, Mass.: D. C. Heath, 1978).

Pages 122–123
Friends of the Earth on transportation shortfall: Steinhart et al., Pathway to Energy Sufficiency, pp. 21–23.

Page 123
Friends of the Earth on parking lots: Ibid., p. 23.
Van der Ryn on suburbs: Sim Van der Ryn, "Ecotopia Now: Utopia Brought Down to Earth," New Age 26 (March 1979), p. 32. On vegetables: Ibid., p. 31. On lawn: Ibid., p. 32. On streets: Ibid.

Page 124
The case for energy savings through centralization: Bruce Hannon, "Energy Use and Land Use," in R. Burchell and D. Listokin, eds., Future Land Use (New Brunswick, N.J.: Center for Urban Policy Research, 1981); and Kirkpatrick Sale, Human Scale (New York: Coward, McCann, and Geohegan, 1980). Hannon calls for the development of small governmental units, but within the context of spatial concentration.
On the savings from weatherizing: See Owen Phillips, The Last Chance Energy Book (Baltimore: Johns Hopkins Press, 1979).

Page 125
On classical knowledge of passive solar design: See Borimir Jordan and John Perlin, "Solar Energy Use and Litigation in Ancient Times," Solar Law Reporter 1 (September/October 1979), pp. 583–594.
On the coming of photovoltaics: See Paul D. Maycock and Edward N. Stirewalt, Photovoltaics: Sunlight to Electricity in One Step (Andover, Mass.: Brick House Publishing Co., 1981); and J. Richard Burke, "Photovoltaics: Down to Earth at Last," The SERI Journal (Spring 1981), pp. 4–13. A list of thirty-eight publications on photovoltaics by the Solar Energy Research Institute (SERI) is found on page 38 of the same issue of The SERI Journal.
David Morris on General Electric's shingle: Comments at the Second Conference on Community Renewable Energy Systems sponsored by the Solar Energy Research Institute and held in Seattle (September 3–5, 1980).
Rifkin on the return to the farm: Jeremy Rifkin, Entropy (New York: Viking, 1980), p. 216.

Page 126
Rifkin on the limits of solar resources: Ibid., p. 199.

On group life under collective conditions: See Rosabeth Moss Kanter, *Commitment and Community: Communes and Utopias in Sociological Perspective* (Cambridge, Mass.: Harvard University Press, 1972).

Page 127
Amory Lovins takes a more optimistic position on the possibility of maintaining personal transport habits by the provision of grain and wood alcohol. He envisages a mobile solar future in which

> the amount of transport required to gain desired access, like the amount of energy required to perform desired tasks, can be reduced by technical and structural changes, but nonetheless the diversity of settlement patterns and lifestyles in a pluralistic society will yield a spectrum of transport densities needed. It is the hard path, with its bias toward homogeneity and large scale, that is ideologically rigid, and the soft path, with its emphasis on appropriateness to the task at hand, that represents a flexible, pluralistic social fabric. [Amory Lovins, *Soft Energy Paths: Toward a Durable Peace* (New York: Harper Colophon, 1977), pp. 102–103.]

On the food-fuel controversy: See Lester R. Brown, "Food or Fuel: New Competition for the World's Cropland," *Worldwatch* paper 35 (Washington, D.C.: The Worldwatch Institute, 1980).
Pollock on the solar city: Peter Lewis Pollock, "Direct Use of Solar Energy in the Compact City" (Golden, Colo.: Solar Energy Research Institute, 1980).

Page 128
Ralph Knowles and Richard Berry, *Solar Envelope Concepts: Moderate Density Applications* (Golden, Colo.: Solar Energy Research Institute, 1980).
Murray Milne, M. Adelson, and R. Corwin, *Three Urban Solar Futures: Characterization of a Future Community Under Three Energy-Supply Scenarios* (Washington, D.C.: Department of Energy, 1979).
Van der Ryn on water conservation: Sim Van der Ryn, *The Toilet Papers: Design for Dry Toilets, Grey Water Systems, and Recycling Human Wastes* (Santa Barbara, Calif.: Capra Press, 1978).

Page 129
"Another study . . .": Robert Twiss and associates as part of the Technology Assessment of Solar Energy Project reported in Ronald L. Ritschard, *Assessment of Solar Energy Within a Community: Summary*

of Three Community-Level Studies (Berkeley: Lawrence Berkeley Laboratory,1979).

Jaffee on visual intrusion of solar equipment: Martin Jaffee, discussion at Second Conference on Community Renewable Energy Systems sponsored by the Solar Energy Research Institute and held in Seattle (September 3–5, 1980).

"Fewer than one-tenth of 1 percent": Donald Aitken, speech to the Second Conference on Community Renewable Energy Systems sponsored by the Solar Energy Research Institute and held in Seattle (September 3–5, 1980).

CHAPTER 7

Pages 134–135

Rich on coproduction: Richard C. Rich, "Municipal Service and the Interaction of the Voluntary and Government Sectors," *Administration and Society* 13 (May 1981), pp. 59–76.

Page 136

Reports on Carbondale, Illinois, and Santa Clara County, California: Presented to the Second Conference on Community Renewable Energy Systems sponsored by Solar Energy Research Institute and held in Seattle (September 3–5, 1980).

Robert Stobaugh and Daniel Yergin, eds., *Energy Future: Report of the Energy Project at the Harvard Business School,* rev. ed. (New York: Ballantine, 1980), p. 139.

Page 138

Dr. LaMar and the windmill: Article in the *Courier-Post* of Camden County, N.J. (November 2, 1980).

Page 139

Hess on community technology: Karl Hess, *Community Technology* (New York: Harper Colophon, 1979), pp. 98–99.

Hess on new technology: *Ibid.,* p. 100.

Stokes on the transition: Bruce Stokes, *Helping Ourselves: Local Solutions to Global Problems* (New York: W. W. Norton, 1981), p. 49. My chapter in this work parallels Chapter 3 (The Consumer Energy Resource) in Stokes's book at a number of points, particularly in its discussion of the consumer as energy producer.

Page 140
Hess's vision: *Community Technology,* p. 107.

Page 141
For a full description of how a just and productive society based on energy decentralization might work, see David Morris and Karl Hess, *Neighborhood Power* (Boston: Beacon Press, 1975).

On the limits of citizen participation: See Barry Checkoway and Jon Van Til, "What Do We Know About Citizen Participation? A Selective Review of Research," in Stuart Langton, ed., *Citizen Participation in America* (Lexington, Mass.: Lexington Books, 1978), pp. 25–42.

Page 142
On the failure of many forms of citizen action to provide direct payoffs to participants: See Mancur Olson, *The Logic of Collective Action* (Cambridge, Mass.: Harvard University Press, 1965).

CHAPTER 8

Page 147
On self-help: See Alan Gartner and Frank Riessman, *Self-Help in the Human Services* (New York: Jossey-Bass, 1978).

On voluntary action: See Jon Van Til, "In Search of Volunt. . .ism," *Volunteer Administration* 12 (Summer 1979), pp. 8–20; David Horton Smith and associates, *Voluntary Action Research 1972* (and 1973, 1974) (Lexington, Mass.: D. C. Heath); and the *Journal of Voluntary Action Research.*

Page 148
Olsen on energy conservation: Marvin E. Olsen, "Public Acceptance of Energy Conservation," in Seymour Warkov, ed., *Energy Policy in the United States: Social and Behavioral Dimensions* (New York: Praeger, 1978), pp. 91–109; Marvin E. Olsen and Bernward Joerges, "The Process of Promoting Consumer Energy Conservation: An International Perspective," (Berlin, The International Institute for Environment and Society of the Science Center Berlin, 1981).

Page 149
Olsen on the reality of the energy problem: "Public Acceptance of Energy Conservation," p. 91.

Survey data reported in this chapter come from the following sources:

Council on Environmental Quality (CEQ) et al., *Public Opinion on Environmental Issues*, (Washington, D.C.: Government Printing Office, 1980).

Joye J. Dillman, Kenneth R. Tremblay, Jr., and Don A. Dillman, "Energy Policies Directed at the Home: Which Ones Will People Accept?" *Housing Educators Journal* 4 (1977), pp. 2–13.

Bonnie Maas Morrison, Joanne Goodman Keith, and James J. Zuiches, "Impacts on Household Energy Consumption: An Empirical Study of Michigan Families," in C. T. Unseld et al., eds., *Sociopolitical Effects of Energy Use and Policy*, Supporting Paper 5, Study of Nuclear and Alternative Energy Systems (Washington, D.C.: National Academy of Sciences, 1979), pp. 7–33.

Jeffrey S. Milstein, "How Consumers Feel About Energy: Attitudes and Behavior During the Winter and Spring 1976–77," in Warkov, ed., *Energy Policy in the United States*, pp. 79–90.

Al Richman, "The Polls: Public Attitudes toward the Energy Crisis," *Public Opinion Quarterly* 43 (Winter 1979), pp. 576–585.

George H. Gallup, ed., *The Gallup Poll: Public Opinion 1979* (and 1980) (Wilmington, Del.: Scholarly Resources, Inc., 1980 and 1981).

Survey on imports: Richman, "The Polls," p. 579.

Olsen on seriousness of energy problem: Olsen, "Public Acceptance of Energy Conservation," in Warkov, ed., *Energy Policy*, p. 94.

Page 150

August 1979 poll: Gallup.

Shortages as contrived; Roper polls cited by Richman, "The Polls," p. 577.

Agree with President Carter?: CBS/*The New York Times* polls in *Ibid.*

Steady attribution of seriousness: Gallup (1979).

Milstein on 1977 survey on long-term seriousness: Milstein, "How Consumers Feel About Energy," in Warkov, ed., *Energy Policy*, p. 87.

Michigan sample: Morrison, "Impacts on Household Energy Consumption," in Unseld et al., eds., *Sociopolitical Effects*, p. 15.

Page 151

Richman on public concern about world oil supplies: Richman, "The Polls," p. 578.

Mid–1979 sample on foreign oil needs: Roper, in *Ibid.*, p. 579.

Seven percent not optimistic: Harris polls, in *Ibid.*, p. 581.

Olsen on minimal effort: Olsen, "Public Acceptance of Energy Conservation," in Warkov, ed., *Energy Policy,* p. 94.

Washington heating limits: Dillman et al., "Energy Policies Directed at the Home," p. 6.

Page 152

List of energy choices: CEQ et al., *Public Opinion on Environmental Issues,* p. 22.

Olsen on minimal savings: Olsen, "Public Acceptance of Energy Conservation," in Warkov, ed., *Energy Policy,* p. 94.

Among the indicators that conservation has taken a firm hold on American life ways, as of 1981, are

- A 20 percent decline in the consumption of heating oil between 1972 and 1978
- An 18 percent decline in the use of natural gas over the same period
- A 7.7 percent decline in gasoline consumption from the first three quarters of 1980 to the same portion of the previous year
- A decline in imported oil to 6.7 million barrels a day in 1980 from its peak, near 9 million barrels per day in 1979.

Source: "Gains in Saving Oil Change U.S. Outlook," *The New York Times* (January 4, 1981).

Recent conservation findings: Gallup polls (1979, 1980).

Solar installation intentions: CEQ et al., *Public Opinion on Environmental Issues,* pp. 21, 23.

Page 153

Olsen on socioeconomic status: Olsen, "Public Acceptance of Energy Conservation," in Warkov, ed., *Energy Policy,* p. 95.

Olsen on education, occupation, and age: *Ibid.,* p. 95.

Page 154

Milstein on 1977 findings on energy policies: Milstein, "How Consumers Feel About Energy," in Warkov, ed., *Energy Policy,* pp. 83–88.

Page 155

Roper on oil shortages: Summarized in Richman, "The Polls," p. 578.

Page 156

Resources for the Future Study: in CEQ et al., *Public Opinion on Environmental Issues,* p. 23.

Milstein on 1977 nuclear support: Milstein, "How Consumers Feel About Energy," in Warkov, ed., *Energy Policy*, p. 88.

Twenty-nine percent willing to accept health risk: Morrison, "Impacts on Household Energy Consumption," in Unseld et al., eds., *Sociopolitical Effects*, p. 27.

Poll on nuclear safety, 1979: CEQ et al, *Public Opinion on Environmental Issues*, p. 23.

Roper on length of remaining oil supplies: in Richman, "The Polls," p. 579.

Page 157

John M. Darley, Clive Seligman, and Lawrence J. Becker, "The Lesson of Twin Rivers: Feedback Works," *Psychology Today* 12 (April 1979), p. 24.

Page 159

Johnson on muddling: Warren Johnson, *Muddling Toward Frugality: A Blueprint for Survival in the 1980s* (Boulder, Colo.: Shambhala, 1979), p. 237.

Business Week reviewer: Michael G. Sheldrick, "Watching the World Run Out of Resources," *Business Week* (September 8, 1980), pp. 12, 17.

Vacca and Hobbes: Roberto Vacca, *The Coming Dark Age* (Garden City, N.Y.: Doubleday, 1973).

For a detailed analysis of the monopolistic structure of the energy industry, see Lawrence Solomon, *Energy Shock: After the Oil Runs Out* (Toronto: Doubleday Canada Limited, 1980). In addition to tracing the history and present power of energy monopolies, Solomon details the implications of this situation on contemporary patterns of disease, poverty, inflation, and inequality.

Page 160

Candidate Reagan's remarks are taken from *The New York Times* (July 18, 1980).

Page 161

Neal Hatcher has organized "Solar Co-ops" in southern New Jersey for the New Jersey Solar Coalition. A similar movement is being facilitated in Philadelphia by the Institute for the Study of Civic Values.

Page 162

Goodwyn on populism: Lawrence Goodwyn, *The Populist Mo-*

ment (New York: Oxford University Press, 1978).

A personal note: While revising this chapter, I read for the first time Marilyn Ferguson's remarkable study of contemporary transformation movements, *The Aquarian Conspiracy: Personal and Social Transformation in the 1980s* (Los Angeles: J. P. Tarcher, 1980). I was struck by the similarity between the conclusion of her book and the conclusion of my chapter. Marilyn Ferguson writes:

> One by one, we can re-choose—to awaken. To leave the prison of our conditioning, in love, to turn homeward. To conspire with and for each other.
> Awakening brings its own assignments, unique to each of us, chosen by each of us. Whatever you may think about yourself and however long you may have thought it, you are not just you. You are a seed, a silent promise. You are the conspiracy. [p. 417]

I have left my conclusion unrevised, despite what some might find too close a resemblance to Ferguson in theme and style. It stands as evidence, at least for me, of the reality of the quiet movement toward a rational, humane, and peaceful energy future. The "Aquarian Conspiracy" exists!

Index